COOL MILLION

HOW TO BECOME A
MILLION DOLLAR SCREENWRITER

COOL MILLION

HOW TO BECOME A
MILLION DOLLAR SCREENWRITER

Sheldon Woodbury

M. Evans and Company, Inc.
New York

M. Evans and Company, Inc.
216 East 49th Street
New York, New York 10017

Library of Congress Cataloguing-in-Publication Data

Woodbury, Sheldon.
   Cool Million : How to Become a Million Dollar Screenwriter / Sheldon
Woodbury.
   p. cm.
Includes index
ISBN 1-59077-018-8 (pbk.)
1. Motion picture authorship. I. Title
   PN1996.W64 2003
   808.2'3--dc22

                                        2003016425

Typesetting and graphics by Evan Johnston
Printed in the United States of America

10 9 8 7 6 5 4 3 2 1

To LuAnn and William, my wife and my son.
If our life was a movie we'd all be sitting in the
theater watching a dream that suddenly came true.

&

To my parents, my heroes.

CONTENTS

PART 1: IT ALL STARTS WITH A BIG IDEA

PART 2: WHAT YOU NEED TO KNOW ABOUT THE AUDIENCE

PART 3: WRITING A MILLION DOLLAR SCREENPLAY

PART 4: WHAT YOU NEED TO KNOW ABOUT HOLLYWOOD

ACKNOWLEDGMENTS

It's been a wonderful surprise how helpful and generous people have been in supporting this book from the very beginning.

First was D.B. Gilles, my great friend and writing partner, who helped in every way possible. A big thank you and deep appreciation also go to Jane Dystel and Stacey Glick, my agents. Stacey, especially, was instrumental in developing the idea and worked very hard finding *Cool Million* a home.

The amazing PJ Dempsey, my editor, was also responsible for improving *Cool Million* far beyond its original concept. Thanks also to Matt Harper for his smart and insightful suggestions, and Evan Johnston for his terrific book design.

I am also grateful to many others who helped along the way: Lydia and Joan Wilen, authors of *How to Sell Your Screenplay*; Lew Hunter, author of *Lew Hunter's Screenwriting 434*; Howard Meibach of hollywoodlitsales.com; Robert Honor at New York University; Jeff Mehlman; Beth Uffner; Linda Hoffman at Warner Bros.; Glynis Lynn at Phantom Four Productions; and Noah Gallico at the Broder-Kurland-Webb-Uffner Agency.

I also want to thank all my colleagues and students in the Department of Dramatic Writing at New York University for creating a place where movies and screenwriting are treasured and loved.

Thanks also to my mythic and terrific brothers and sister: Marion, Frank, Spencer, and Alice. We grew up watching movies together in the basement of our house in Summit, New Jersey. It was our first blockbuster movie theater.

Lastly, I want to thank all the screenwriters and movie professionals who contributed their time and energy to be interviewed for this book. Without exception, they brought honesty, insight, and passion to every question that was asked. They all interrupted very busy schedules, simply because they wanted to help beginning screenwriters. Their contribution is the heart and soul of the book. I am enormously grateful for their participation.

Finally, to Natalie, Rudi, Mariel, Hunter, Bryson, Payton, Libby, Tate, Chelsea, Tyler, Tara, Noelle, and William:

I hope all your blockbuster dreams
will always come true.

INTRODUCTION

So you want to be a million dollar screenwriter? If your answer is yes, then this book was written specifically for you.

It's also why *Cool Million* is so different from all the other screenwriting books that are available—it's about both the art and business of becoming a successful screenwriter. Most screenwriting books focus only on the craft of screenwriting and leave it at that. They teach you how to write a well-constructed screenplay, then consider the job done.

But in the world of Hollywood screenwriting today, it's a hard and inescapable fact of survival that you can't successfully practice your art without also knowing how the business works. Because "the business of Hollywood" will be the biggest influence on your screenwriting career.

Cool Million was inspired by my experiences as both a screenwriter and a screenwriting teacher. As a screenwriter, I've come to realize how important it is to be smart and educated about how the movie industry works. If you want to write screenplays that get made into movies, it's absolutely essential to understand why some movies get made and others don't.

As a screenwriting teacher in the Department of Dramatic Writing at New York University's Tisch School of the Arts, I also work with some of the most talented young screenwriters in the country, and I see first-hand the pressures they have to face. They've decided to pursue an artistic career that's immediately filled with challenges. Their parents are usually less than enthusiastic, and their confidence level is usually a bit shaky, too. But like students in any other top-level college program, they're not only smart and talented, they're also ambitious. They want to be successful. They want to be the best. They desperately want their professional dreams to come true.

That's why Cool Million *is ambitious, too.*

It won't just teach you how to write a screenplay; it will teach you how to write a screenplay that movie audiences and Hollywood will both love. The book is specifically designed to give you the knowledge and skills you'll need to build a career as a million dollar screenwriter.

Interviews with a top Hollywood agent and studio executive will reveal exactly what the movie industry looks for in a million dollar screenplay. The book also includes in-depth interviews with eleven top million dollar screenwriters, who will share their insider secrets and give expert advice on all aspects of the business. The screenwriters were all unflinchingly honest, not holding back on revealing the highs and lows of being paid millions for what's inside their heads.

What you'll learn from the interviews is that a million screenwriter can be anybody. One went to Stanford. Another is a college dropout. One started out writing jokes for the comedian Jimmy Walker in high school. Another wanted to be a homicide detective. One got his big break working as a chauffeur for a movie director. The screenwriters interviewed are all as different as the movies they write, but they all share one thing in common: *success*.

My only regret is that I wasn't able to include a female screenwriter in the book. I tried very hard. So if you're an aspiring female screenwriter, please don't let that diminish your ambition. There are many million dollar female screenwriters, but there's always room for more.

Finally, before we begin, let's all agree on a very important artistic belief that's another fundamental inspiration for this book.

Making a million dollars for what's inside your head is cool!

HOW THIS BOOK WORKS

Cool Million is organized to be both easy-to-use and compre-hensive in scope. For best use of the book, it's also strongly recommended that you read it from beginning to end and not jump around and only read selectively.

Cool Million is Divided into Four Parts. These broad sections are arranged to take you sequentially through the steps involved in writing and selling a screenplay. They cover everything from the beginning creative process (finding the idea, creating the story), to the craft of screenwriting (writing style, story structure), to how to crack the Hollywood market. The focus at every step will be on how to write a million dollar screenplay and how to become a million dollar screenwriter.

Blockbuster Advice. This is a section that comes at the end of chapters where the million dollar screen-writers give their insights and advice. Using their own movies and careers as examples, the screenwriters reveal their personal secrets and tips on the topics just covered. They don't always agree on every topic, but that's useful, too, for choosing the advice that works best for you.

Movie Close-Ups. There's no better way to learn how to write movies than from the movies themselves. The movie close-ups are smaller sections in the chapters that use well known movies to illustrate key screenwriting techniques.

From Idea to Million Dollar Sale. From the first light bulb going off in the screenwriter's head to the final big-money sale, these chapter inserts will show how some of the screenwriters made their most exciting million dollar screenplay sales.

A Blockbuster Beginning. This chapter insert highlights the unusual way one blockbuster screenwriter found a way into the business. David Hayter, the screenwriter of *X-Men*, put himself in the right place at the right time. Breaking in is one of the

toughest challenges a beginning screenwriter faces and this personal story shows how you have to be ready when opportunity appears.

Industry Interviews. Because understanding the movie business is so essential to writing screenplays that sell and get made into movies, these interviews with top Hollywood players give you the straight scoop on what Hollywood wants.

THE SCREENWRITERS

DAVID BENIOFF has become one of the hottest screenwriters in Hollywood in the last few years, with several high-profile projects in various stages of development.He adapted his novel, *The 25th Hour*, which Spike Lee directed. His spec script, *Stay*, sold for a record $1.8 million. His original screenplay, *Troy*, is in development with Wolfgang Peterson as director and Brad Pitt as the star.

NEAL BRENNAN is a young comedy screenwriter who had his first screenplay, *Half Baked*, produced when he was only twenty-two years old. Since then, in just a few years, he's gone on to sell two big-money screenplays, *Totally Awesome* and *The Oldest Living Man In The World*.

PHILIP EISNER began his screenwriting career with a four-picture deal at Largo Entertainment. He's written movie projects for Robert DeNiro's Tribeca Productions, TriStar, The Jim Henson Company, and others. His original script, *Event Horizon*, a mind-bending combination of science-fiction and horror, was produced by Paramount Pictures and directed by Paul Anderson.

AKIVA GOLDSMAN is considered one of the very best and most versatile screenwriters working today. He won the 2001 Academy Award, the Golden Globe award, and the Writer's Guild Award for his spectacular screenplay adaptation of the book *A Beautiful Mind*. His other writing credits include *The Client*, *Batman Forever*, *A Time To Kill*, *Lost In Space*, and *Practical Magic*.

DAVID GOYER writes movies that are filled with style, talent and non-stop imagination. He wrote the screenplay adaptation for *Blade* and *Blade II*, based on the Marvel comic. His other writing credits include screenplays for *The Puppet Masters*, *Crow: City of Angels*, and *Dark City*.

DAVID HAYTER began his career as an actor, then switched to screenwriting. In just a few years, he's already moved to the top ranks of sought after blockbuster screenwriters. He wrote the screenplay for the smash hit *X-Men*, directed by Bryan Singer. He also wrote *The Hulk*, another Marvel comic adaptation. His next project is *Watchmen*, an adaptation of the legendary comic by Alan Moore, as writer and director.

JIM KOUF has been a successful and prolific screenwriter, producer, and director, working in a variety of genres. His many screenplay credits include *The Hidden*, *Class*, *American Dreamer*, *Operation Dumbo Drop*, *Stakeout*, *Rush Hour*, and *Snow Dogs*.

DALE LAUNER has written some of the sharpest and funniest movie comedies to hit the big-screen. His credits include *Love Potion #9*, *Blind Date*, *Ruthless People*, *Dirty Rotten Scoundrels*, and *My Cousin Vinny*. He also sold one of the highest-selling spec scripts of all time, *Bad Dog*, for $3 million.

ANDREW MARLOWE is one of the premier blockbuster screenwriters working today, with a recent string of big-concept, big-budget movies. He wrote *Air Force One* starring Harrison Ford, *Hollow Man*, and *The End of Days*, starring Arnold Schwarzenegger.

SCOTT ROSENBERG is widely considered one of the most versatile, prolific, and mega-talented young screenwriters in Hollywood. He's the writer of *Things to do in Denver When You're Dead*, *Con Air*, *Disturbing Behavior*, *Beautiful Girls*, and *Gone in 60 Seconds*.

ED SOLOMON is one of the top screenwriters in Hollywood. His first big success was co-writing *Bill & Ted's Excellent Adventure*, along with *Bill & Ted's Bogus Journey*. His many writing credits include *Leaving Normal* and *Men In Black*. *Levity*, which he wrote and directed, is his most recent movie.

IMAGINE THIS

You wake up in the morning and stumble out of bed. You make some coffee, read the newspaper for awhile, then walk to the office in your house. You still have your pajamas on, or maybe a pair of old shorts and a t-shirt. There's music in the background.

Meanwhile, outside, all around the city or town where you live, other people are up, too. But most of them are fighting traffic, fighting boredom, or fighting for their jobs. They work in an office where it's dull and dreary, every day like every other. They're secretly crossing off the days on the calendar, waiting for the weekend, their next vacation, and finally retirement.

Not you though.

You turn on your computer and begin to write. Almost immediately you're lost in another world and it's a hundred times more exciting than the world we live in.

There are larger-than-life heroes and despicable villains. There are great battles and adventures, beautiful women.

There are non-stop thrills and surprises, action and danger. Maybe it's taking place in the farthest reaches of outer space, or deep inside the Earth, or in a spectacular new landscape that's magical and mystical.

You spend the morning getting more and more excited because you're coming to the end. You're writing a screenplay, and it's finally finished.

That afternoon you send it off to your agent.

Then, a week later, you suddenly get even more excited. Your agent calls and tells you your screenplay just sold for a million dollars.

Guess what?

It happens.

Now imagine this.

It happens to you.

PART ONE

IT ALL STARTS WITH A BIG IDEA

chapter 1

THAT'S A LOT OF MONEY— WHO ARE THESE PEOPLE?

"No job too big, no fee too big."
—Ghostbusters

To define what a million dollar screenwriter is, you first need to understand how the whole business of movies has changed in recent years. Over the last two decades, making movies has grown increasingly more sophisticated and complicated. It's also grown more profitable, competitive, and market driven.

Movies have become a mega-million dollar industry where the potential risks and rewards are both colossal. A hit movie can mean hundreds of millions in profit and dizzy acclaim for the people involved. A big misfire, on the other hand, can instantly cause melt-down to reputations, careers, and movie-studio balance sheets.

Because of this, in the last fifteen or so years, studios have put more emphasis on a single creative entity that can make it all happen.

THE BLOCKBUSTER SCREENPLAY

With a great screenplay, every player in Hollywood knows the sky is the limit. It starts the whole process rolling, attracting the talent and generating studio excitement. And finally, if the audience loves it, the movie becomes a hit and everybody wins.

We'll call this a "blockbuster screenplay." A blockbuster screenplay delivers a movie story that has terrific commercial appeal. It's a story that can attract and entertain the widest possible audience.

We'll also call million dollar screenwriters "blockbuster screenwriters" and hit movies "blockbuster movies."

Hollywood is looking for blockbuster screenplays because agents, directors, producers, and studio executives know that having one is the essential first step in the pursuit of box-office gold. And this is fundamental to what a million dollar screenwriter is. They write a screenplay Hollywood believes can be a hit movie.

TWO KINDS OF MILLION DOLLAR SCREENWRITERS

The Million Dollar "Spec"

A spec screenplay is one that a screenwriter writes entirely on his or her their own without any kind of contract or assignment. They're called "spec screenplays" because they're written on speculation.

It can be a first-time screenwriter living far away from the glitter of Hollywood while working as a school teacher, a housewife, a cop, or anything else. It can also be a professional screenwriter who's between jobs, has a great idea, and wants to take a shot in the spec market.

When a studio or producer buys a spec script, they don't care about the identity of the screenwriter. The buyer reads the screenplay and sees something in the story that he or she believes will attract and connect with movie-goers.

An example of a young screenwriter who had great success in the spec market is Shane Black. He sold his first produced screenplay, *Lethal Weapon*, when he was twenty-two years old. A few years later, he sold *The Last Boy Scout* for $1.7 million. A few years after that, he sold *The Long Kiss Goodnight* for $4.6 million.

In all three cases, he wrote the screenplays without any kind of deal or payment. When you're writing a spec screenplay, you're betting it will be a winner and someone will buy it. Sometimes they do and sometimes they don't. That's the gamble.

For Shane Black, the gamble paid off for all three screenplays because they were all great stories, with spectacular visual action; a dark, funhouse plot; and edgy, entertaining characters.

They all sold for a lot of money, because at the time, they where sharper, faster and funnier than anything in the same genre that had come before. They were the kind of movies audiences love. Which is why there's also been a *Lethal Weapon 2, 3*, and *4*.

Another young screenwriter who hit it big in the spec market is M. Night Shyamalan. Following the success of *The Sixth Sense*, he sold his spec screenplay *Unbreakable* for $5 million and received another $5 million for directing.

Joe Eszterhas is considered the king of million dollar screenplay sales. He sold a one-page outline for the movie *One Night Stand* for $4 million dollars. His mythic bio also includes the $2 million he got for *Showgirls* after he scribbled the story on the back of a napkin.

The Blockbuster Pro

The second kind of million dollar screenwriter is the proven veteran who can command a million dollars or more for their services. This can happen in a variety of ways. One type of assignment is when they're contracted by a studio or a producer to write a screenplay based on another work—a novel, play, television show, etc. Another is when they're hired to write a screenplay from an idea, or rewrite a screenplay that's already been written.

The reason this select group of screenwriters receives top dollar is because they've already written movies that have been successful. They've proved they can create and write a movie story audiences will love.

WHY THEY'RE PAID THE BIG BUCKS

These top level screenwriters are the go-to people that executives and producers trust and depend on, from the big-sale beginner to the top-level professional. Through either specs or assignments, they've earned this position by writing well-crafted screenplays geared to a big commercial audience. They create movie stories people want to see, and the industry recognizes this and rewards them with a big paycheck. Making a big budget movie means rolling very expensive dice, so the screenwriters who've proven they can deliver are at the top of the pay scale.

In the treasure-hunt search for a blockbuster movie, the bonanza can begin with the screenwriter.

So if you're a beginning screenwriter with blockbuster-dreams, you need to begin with a belief based on fact.

It can happen.

Starting Out

As a beginning screenwriter, you can start your career anywhere; it really doesn't matter.

As the following illustrates, blockbuster screenwriters come from many different starting points and backgrounds. There's no one way to do it, or agreed-on set of rules to follow. Some of the interviewed screenwriters even started out with a entirely different kind of career goal, while others pursued their screenwriting dream from the very beginning.

As you'll see though, you already share something with our million dollar screenwriters. They all started out just like you, an unknown with nothing more than a burning desire to work in the movies.

DAVID BENIOFF *(The 25th Hour)*

I grew up in New York City, but I got my master's degree in Irish literature from Trinity College in Dublin. I became a screenwriter by accident. I wanted to be a novelist. I'm still very inspired by Ernest Hemingway and Samuel Beckett. Both have very pared down prose with strong characters and stories.

I wrote three novels. The first I never submitted to anybody. The second was turned down by everybody. But the second one got me my agent. And the third, *The 25th Hour*, sold after a long time, after a lot of rejection.

One of the book galleys for *The 25th Hour* was sent to Tobey McGuire's production company. He liked it and optioned it.

Because I was living in Los Angeles, I went to meet with them, and they hired me to write the adaptation. That was great, because I didn't want anybody else messing around with it. I'd never written a screenplay by myself. I'd written a horror script with a friend, but that was it.

NEIL BRENNAN *(Half Baked)*

I grew up as the youngest of ten kids in Chicago. One of my oldest brothers, Kevin Brennan, is a comedian, and that was a big influence on me. I used to visit him in New York. That was a huge-eye opener, being around other comedians and creative people. It was great.

In high school I was interested in being a comedy performer, an actor. So I would write jokes because that's what I was interested in. I used to watch all the stand-up comedy shows that were on TV that were popular then. My brother was on a lot of them, so it was cool.

PHILIP EISNER *(Event Horizon)*

I grew up in Fort Worth, Texas. I was never interested in being a screenwriter. I was a theater geek in high school. But I'd always written. And I loved movies.

For me, *Star Wars* just blew the lid off what you can make a movie about. I loved *Alien* and *Aliens*. But the movie that inspired me the most was *The Road Warrior*. I remember I rented the video and there was an ice storm, so I couldn't return it for four days. I watched the entire film in slow motion, and that's my education on how to make an action movie.

AKIVA GOLDSMAN *(A Beautiful Mind)*

I was born in Brooklyn Heights, New York. Both my parents were child psychologists. Most of all, I grew up loving movies. I loved staying up late watching science fiction movies on television.

My formal education is from Wesleyan as an undergraduate, then NYU, where I got my master's in fiction writing. I had these extraordinary writing teachers: Ed Doctorow, Russell Banks, Margaret Atwood, and Gordon Lish. As a fiction writer, I was okay, not great. Fiction writing is something that I greatly admire, but I was also beginning to realize that it was something I was never going to master. I'm still in awe of a great short story.

DAVID GOYER *(Blade)*

I'm from Ann Arbor, Michigan. In my senior year in high school, I was originally thinking about getting a degree in police administration and becoming a homicide detective.

Screenwriting was kind of a fluke. At the time, growing up, the idea of someone from Michigan going to Hollywood and becoming a screenwriter seemed so remote and non-existent. But when I was a kid, I loved all the science-fiction and monster movies. I'd watch them after school. Movies like *The Omega Man*, *Logan's Run* and *Rollerball*. They look a little cheesy now, but I loved them.

DAVID HAYTER *(X-Men)*

I never intended to be a screenwriter. I came to Los Angeles to be an actor. I had always written though. I wrote in my spare time to help me understand the moviemaking process better and because I wanted to know why movies that should have been good weren't, and why movies that seemed like they shouldn't work did. I did it to understand filmmaking in a broader sense. I started reading screenwriting books and writing short scripts. When I was twenty-seven and frustrated with my career, myself and another actor friend put together a movie and starred in it. I completely backed into screenwriting. My first professional job was *X-Men*.

JIM KOUF *(Rush Hour)*

I grew up making movies as a kid. I loved it. I grew up in a neighborhood in California where movie people lived. Some of my friends had parents who were actors, cameramen, editors, etc. I started writing little films and shooting them with my friends on an 8 mm or 16 mm camera.

ANDREW MARLOWE *(Air Force One)*

I was born in Thailand. Both my parents were cultural anthropologists. When I was one, we moved back to the United States. I grew up in Silver Springs, Maryland.

My parents did this thing when I was growing up called "movie night." They'd get films from the local library and show them on this beat up 16 mm projector. So I got to see Bergman, Preston Sturgis and Billy Wilder in my living room. The group that came over were all academics. They'd have wine and cheese and talk about the movies. So I feel like I started my education by osmosis at a very young age.

I majored in English, with a philosophy minor, at Columbia University in New York City. After Columbia, I was a PA on a low-budget movie. It was a great experience, because I got to see everything. But I also realized that if I wanted to be on set, I wanted to be running things, not just getting up at 5 a.m. to make coffee.

After that, I got a job with a literary agency in New York. When I was there I started reading the stuff that was coming in from clients and those wanting to break into the business.

I started thinking that this was something I could do. I had always been interested in screenwriting, but being at the agency and reading other people's stuff really crystallized it.

SCOTT ROSENBERG *(Con Air)*

I grew up in Boston and went to Boston University. I wrote a lot of short stories in college. I was a communications major, but I got into the Graduate Fiction department as a sophomore, which was very cool. Writing was the one thing I did well. My original plan was to go to Europe and write novels. I liked the whole notion of smoking hash in Amsterdam and writing novels.

But when I graduated, this girl I really liked moved to California and I just followed her out there. If you write and you're in Los Angeles, eventually you're going to start writing screenplays. I was doing shit jobs. One of my first jobs was selling cookbooks, and I had to dress in a chef's hat. It was brutal. I drove a truck for awhile, too, but I was always writing at night. I would come home to this shit apartment. We didn't even have a desk. I would put a portable Smith-Corona typewriter on my lap. I was writing six or seven scripts a year at night. When you're young, it's important you use that energy level.

ED SOLOMON *(Men in Black)*

I was raised in a small-town in Massachusetts. I always wanted to write. I didn't know about writing movies, I just wanted to write. When I was nineteen I got a job as a joke writer for comedians. The first person I sold jokes to was Jimmy Walker, who was in the TV show *Good Times*.

When I was growing up, I didn't watch movies that much. I didn't even read that much. I wish I'd read a lot more. I liked the Woody Allen movies and the Mel Brooks movies and the Monty Python movies. They probably influenced me a lot. But I didn't go to movies that much, and I still don't. There just aren't that many really good movies.

BLOCKBUSTER MOVIES ARE BIG IN EVERY WAY

*"This thing is much too big to
be some lost dinosaur."*
—Godzilla

Blockbuster movies are first and foremost . . . BIG. They're giant pictures glowing on a very big screen. That's one of the reasons they affect us in such an intense, thrilling, and powerful way. It's probably why you're reading this book. At some point in your life, movies have touched you, and that memory is still very special. In fact, right now, in your head, I'm sure there are movies you can remember as clearly as meories that come from your own life.

Try it.

Close your eyes and remember a movie you love.

Maybe it's Star *Wars*, and you see Luke Skywalker in his starfighter blasting across the jagged surface of the Deathstar, and he hears the soft voice of Obi-Wan Kenobi telling him what to do: "Use the force, Luke." Or it's *Jaws* and you see the scene at the beginning of the movie, when the blonde-haired girl wanders away from the beach party for a late night swim and she's suddenly snatched from sight and dragged below by something big and powerful.

Whatever movie it is, you can see these images in your mind as clearly as memories that come from your own life. That's because they are a part of your life. Once you've seen them, they're a part of who you are.

All story mediums have their own special strengths, whether it's sitting around a campfire listening to a ghost story, curling up with a good book, or watching your favorite show on TV. Each has the ability to entertain and touch us.

But movies are truly unique.

They're a communal gathering, and they take place in the dark. As we sit quietly with friends and strangers, giant glowing images begin to flash and flicker in front of us. Our eyes and brains take in the colossal pictures, and it's like watching our secret dreams and wildest flights of imagination made real. We munch popcorn and slurp down sodas, leaving our everyday lives behind. Within seconds, we're off on a shared two-hour-rollercoaster-big-screen-adventure. It might be into outer space to explore new wonders, or off to a remote unknown island to frolic with dinosaurs, or even down a secret tunnel into a famous actor's mind. But it's all completely and utterly real, because it's all happening right there in front of us on that giant glowing screen. It's bigger than life, grand and majestic.

That brings us to the first step to writing a blockbuster screenplay, which is thinking big, too, and finding a big idea.

Not a mediocre idea.

Or even a pretty good idea.

A BIG IDEA.

MILLION DOLLAR SCREENPLAYS START WITH A BIG IDEA

If you want to write a blockbuster screenplay, this is the first step. It comes before you create your characters or begin thinking about the plot. But it's not only the first step, it's also the most important step.

Without a big idea, it's impossible to write a screenplay that will excite producers and studio executives enough to gamble big money. The reason a big idea is so important is because producers and studio executives know it's the single most important element that attracts an audience. Audiences decide whether or not to go to a movie based on it's overall concept. It's not the intricate nuances of the plot or the snappy dialogue between characters. Audiences see a newspaper ad, or a commercial on TV that communicates the main concept of the movie, then make a decision based on that.

A big idea is the foundation for your blockbuster movie. It's what makes your movie story unique and special. If you want to write a million dollar screenplay you have to build the story on an idea that's big enough and bold enough to excite both a huge audience and the Hollywood executives who will buy it.

A big idea can come from anywhere and everywhere, so you have to always be open to inspiration. As a comedy screenwriter, Neal Brennan found a big idea in a place where he might have been tempted to just sit back and enjoy the sights.

FROM IDEA
TO MILLION
DOLLAR $ALE

Neal Brennan

I got this idea when I was at a party and I saw Hugh Hefner. He was like seventy-three at the time, and he had a bunch of bodyguards to protect him. I basically had the whole idea for the movie in eight seconds. It's about a guy who runs a museum in the Midwest for the oldest living man ever. Then they find out there's another guy who's going to be older, and the town sends this young guy on a mission to kill him so they won't lose their museum.

I wrote it with a partner, Michael Shur, who worked for *Saturday Night Live*. I told him the idea and he loved it. We went to Los Angeles for a week and pitched it to over twenty places. Nobody wanted it. We thought we were the biggest losers.

Then on a Friday we pitched it to Disney and they said they'd get back to us. We thought they were lying. Michael went home. On Monday I pitched it to MTV Films by myself. They loved it. I got in my car, still feeling battered from the week, and I called my agent. He said there was already a bidding war. We went with the higher offer, $450,000 against $1 million. It felt great. I was twenty-five years old.

A Big Idea Is Also High Concept

The term "high concept" is Hollywood lingo to describe a movie with a big idea. More specifically, it's a movie idea that's judged to be so commercially appealing it will draw a huge audience all by itself. High concept means high audience appeal. It's the kind of idea that when people hear it, they're immediately excited about seeing the movie. A high-concept idea instantly hooks an audience with its premise. *Honey, I Shrunk the Kids* is a high concept idea. So is *Independence Day* and *The Santa Clause*.

In the business of movies, great high concept screenplays always generate the most buzz. Coming up with a big idea is the same as creating a high-concept idea.

Screenwriting is incredibly competitive for lots of different reasons. One of the main reasons is because you're trying to sell stories to a very expensive machine. It's the movie-making machine that's putting our best dreams and imagination on those giant glowing screens, and it's putting them there so millions of people will spend money to come watch them.

So you have to earn your right to be there.

You do that by coming up with a big idea.

Finding A Big Idea

Beginning your career begins with your movie idea. Many of the screenwriters urge beginning screenwriters to write the kind of movie they'd love to see, as long as it's not something small and personal from their own life.

What separates blockbuster screenwriters from everybody else is their ability to be bigger and bolder. They create stories that transcend what's normal and expected. They have the talent to imagine big new ideas that are thrilling and entertaining.

Inspiration is a highly personal experience and all screenwriters have different methods for conjuring good ideas. As a beginning screenwriter, you need to find out what inspires you and develop a way to evaluate the commercial potential of your movie ideas. Here are how some of the pros begin their writing process.

DAVID BENIOFF *(The 25th Hour)*

I have a lot of different story ideas in my head, and the ones that stay there for a long time are the ones that I like and tend to pursue. That's my test for picking an idea I want to write.

PHILIP EISNER *(Event Horizon)*

I'm inspired by movies. When I came up with the idea for *Event Horizon*, I was inspired by *The Haunting*, *The Shining*, and *The Abyss*. In *The Abyss* I really liked Michael Biehn's character. I was fascinated by a character who was going insane in a hostile environment. And he wasn't evil, he was a good guy. And I kept thinking, what's more terrifying than being trapped deep in the ocean? So I came up with outer space, orbiting around Neptune. Then everything else was being inspired by other "bad place" movies.

I'm also inspired by bad movies. For me, seeing bad movies is great. *The Matrix* is so good on all levels, when you see it, it doesn't leave any room for inspiring new ideas. But when you go see a bad movie, and I love bad movies, there's invariably a brilliant idea. It's the idea that got everybody jazzed to do it. But they blew it. So I'll think, that's a great idea, how can I use it to write a great script.

For me, writing a screenplay is always about, is this something I want to see? Don't write what you know, because nobody knows shit. Don't write that personal story that has you as the hero, because it's not something other people will be interested in. Write what you want to see as a movie. There are some great coming-of-age movies, but when you see them on the screen, those few that actually make it through, they're brilliantly written. They're not just good, they blow your doors off.

I tend to write for myself, but I happen to have very straightforward commercial tastes. I love science-fiction. I love horror films. I love science-fiction horror films.

AKIVA GOLDSMAN (A Beautiful Mind)

Don't try to predict what other people will like. You have to be both sensitive to pleasing others and inured to it. It's a funny combination. Getting that balance right takes time and luck. Nobody knows what the market will bear, and our anticipation of the market is always well behind the coming trend.

So you have to write what you know. But that doesn't mean a personal little story. You can take what you know and transpose it into an environment that might be more appealing to the reader and movie-goer.

I'm not really interested in writing about my life. It's not what I write screenplays about. But the feelings from having lived my life, and having those experiences, are definitely what fuel my screenplays.

DAVID GOYER (Blade)

From a fundamental level, if I come up with an idea, or a notion, I always ask myself, if I were an audience member, would I want to see this movie? Is there a beginning, a middle, and end? It's easy to come up with a beginning.

Your idea has to be able to support a whole story. They say write what you know, but that's not good advice, because a lot of beginning screenwriters will write an autobiographical story, and most people's lives are not interesting enough to be made into movies.

DAVID HAYTER (X-Men)

If I immediately start to see images that I've never seen in movies before, then I start to think it's something I want to do. The more jazzed or energized I get by an idea when I first get it or hear it, the more I feel I can transfer that energy to the audience.

In that sense, I'm thinking about the commercial appeal. If I'm really excited, then I think the audience is going to be excited too.

DALE LAUNER *(My Cousin Vinny)*

When deciding whether or not to develop an idea into a screenplay, I always ask myself a question. If I was just an average Joe, and I was working forty or fifty hours a week, and I'm in my twenties, and I'm going to take a girl out on a date, would I want to see this movie?

ANDREW MARLOWE *(Air Force One)*

I feel like I have very mainstream tastes. I like action, but only when it comes from a character point of view. So I look for a character I'd like to spend time with. Then I think about what's not out there that I'd like to see. It always starts with, "What if . . . "

The question you always have to ask is, will anybody want to see it? Because, ultimately, we're not in this to write something that nobody will want to make into a movie or go see at the movie theater. Screenwriting is not just about expressing your personal emotions. If that's all you want to do, you can save everybody a lot of time and money and keep a journal.

If it's a personal story you want to get onscreen, you'll be competing with the people who are doing *Prince of Tides* and *Moonstruck*. These are people who know their craft, who know how to service the actor and build drama.

If a personal story is that important to you, then you might want to learn the craft of screenwriting a little bit more and have more creative tools in your toolbox to do it.

ED SOLOMON *(X-Men)*

You can write a great story starting anywhere. If you want to write something that sells, if you're a good storyteller, you'll write a good story. If you want to write a personal coming-of-age story, and you're a good storyteller, it'll be good. If you're a bad storyteller, and a bad writer, it'll suck. It's really that simple. It doesn't matter what your intention is. What matters is the craft and art you apply to the process.

BEGIN BY LOOKING IN YOUR HEART

*"I would rather have had one breath
of her hair, one kiss from her
mouth, one touch of her hand, than
an eternity without it."*
—City of Angels

The next three chapters will show how you can find your big idea, through specific techniques and steps designed to help you create the concept for your million dollar screenplay.

We'll also cover the larger challenge of what it takes to be a writer, because that's what this process is also about. Being a screenwriter takes a range of skills, and you'll need to develop them all as you begin your career. So as you start looking for your big idea, also begin focusing on how to use your talents to the best of your ability, because that's always a key part of writing a screenplay with blockbuster potential.

So where do you find your big idea?

The good news is you won't have to look far.

Who you are as a writer is defined by who you are as a person, and that's where you start.

Inside all of us there's an amazing and unique collection of emotions, feelings, thoughts, ideas, and images, and that's where you look for your big idea.

You look in your heart, your mind, and your imagination.

BIG IDEAS COME FROM THE HEART

Why the heart? Because all great stories come from what the writer cares passionately about. It comes from their strongest and most heartfelt emotions.

In life, most of us keep our deepest emotions locked away and only share them with people we trust. Expressing love or some other strong emotion opens us up to being hurt or embarrassed by revealing what we honestly believe in and care about. Most of us wouldn't dream of sharing our inner-most secrets, desires, and fears with a stranger.

That is, unless you're a writer, because then it's part of your job description. You have to search your heart and discover what it is you care about on the deepest level and then have the courage to honestly share it with an audience. Writing a blockbuster movie from the heart is taking what you care about and creating an exhilarating and wildly entertaining story that has your own unique passion and point of view.

EDWARD SCISSORHANDS

MOVIE CLOSE-UP

Lots of us felt like outsiders in high school, if we weren't part of the cool crowd, the rich crowd, the jock crowd, whatever. Maybe you were bullied or spent countless nights lying in bed feeling miserable and alone.

A blockbuster screenwriter is able to take this personal heartache and create a story that dramatizes it in a way that's compelling and powerful.

In the movie *Edward Scissorhands*, the screenwriter Caroline Thompson did exactly this in her story about the emotional pain of being an outcast. It's a movie about the misery and heartbreak a teenager experiences because he's judged by others to be different and strange.

What makes the story so vivid is the strong visual way Edward's identity as an outcast is dramatized. When we first meet Edward, he's living all alone in a gloomy gothic castle on the outskirts of town. He's literally an outsider who's grown up away from normal society. And then we see the even more surprising reason he's different. His hands are giant scissors.

It's a great visual metaphor and story device, because we see Edward's anguish in everything he tries to do, from getting dressed, to eating, to being with other people. The story reveals the painful essence of what it feels like to be an outsider, because when you feel alienated, everything becomes a struggle, even the simplest everyday tasks. And for Edward this pain becomes almost unbearable when he realizes, at the end of the movie, he can't even embrace the woman he loves.

The screenwriter used what was in her heart to write a great movie that touched the audience's hearts too.

As a blockbuster screenwriter, you have to be in touch with your inner feelings about yourself, others, and everything around you. That's the life blood that's going to nourish your story ideas. Writers can never hide from their feelings and emotions. You have to keep up a constant dialogue with yourself about who you are and what you care about.

Here are some tools that will help you explore what's in your heart.

THE WRITER'S JOURNAL

A writer's journal is the best way to insure you have an on-going dialogue with your inner feelings and ideas. This is the place you will record all the private thoughts, striking images, and quirky notions that accumulate as you go about your everyday life. Use your journal, or diary, to honestly write about your feelings and insights. Write about what makes you angry, amazed, overwhelmed, bewildered, or curious about anything and everything.

Your writer's journal is what's keeps your mental and emotional flashlight shined on the world around you.

The only rule is to be as honest as you can. When you're in the process of looking for a big idea, you have to begin by looking at what you care about. What's in your heart? What do you want to say about how you feel that only you can say? Look through your writer's journal and see what themes and emotions are the strongest. These can be used as a springboard to creating a big idea.

ASK YOURSELF QUESTIONS

Along with keeping a journal, another technique for finding a big idea from your heart is to ask yourself questions that will probe and reveal your inner feelings. The following questions are a good place to start.

Here too, the only rule is to challenge yourself to be as honest as you can, because the answers can lead to a big idea that's as unique and interesting as you are.

WHAT DO I BELIEVE TO BE TRUE? We all have beliefs and insights that are personal, interesting, and idiosyncratic. That's something to share in a story. It's especially valuable to share if it's off-the-beaten track, off-the-wall, or likely to shake an audience by it's eyeballs and leave them stumbling out of the theater wonderstruck.

WHAT DO I WANT TO BE TRUE? Blockbuster movies are usually about the extremes of life. And they're almost always about hope and an incredible journey/adventure/ordeal/detour/surprising twist-of-fate that finally, ultimately, right at the last second, when you think all hope is lost . . . leads to a better place. What's that for you?

WHAT DO I HATE OR FEAR? Blockbuster movies also tend to have big heroes and villains. Think about what you want to change/vanquish/expose/wrestle to the ground and stomp on in the world around you. Blockbuster movies are often, on a very fundamental level, good old fashioned gunfights between the good guys and the bad guys. It's always more intense and dramatic with a really despicable bad guy/villain/evil cyborg/giant white shark/wicked witch/homicidal boyfriend/etc.

WHAT DO I FEEL PASSIONATELY ABOUT? The best stories come from a writer who wants to change the world, even if it's one reader or

34

movie-goer at a time. Think about what your hopes and dreams are, what you care about that can become "the heart" of your big idea.

Writing From The Heart
Makes Your Writing Unique

As a screenwriter, especially in the beginning, you have to believe you have something to say that only you can say. You have to write from your heart and from your own unique point of view.

In the following, the screenwriters stress the importance of using your emotions and personality as a way of making your writing distinctive and special.

NEAL BRENNAN *(Half Baked)*

It's always difficult in the beginning. It's sort of embarrassing, because you don't know if you're any good. And you're usually not very good when you start out. If you're a beginning screenwriter, you need a desperate, inner, unquenchable need to succeed. You have to work hard and have a respect for what you're doing.

You also have to bring something personal to the story. You have to develop your own point of view. In comedy it's called the "cult of personality." Every comedian has his own style and voice, and that's what you want as a writer.

A Mike Myers comedy is different from a Farrelly Brothers, who are different from the Zucker Brothers, and so on. It's creating a niche for yourself that's special.

PHILIP EISNER *(Event Horizon)*

You have to love what you're writing. It's a chunk out of your life. *Event Horizon* was a year out of my life. If I didn't love the idea and the story, it wouldn't have been worth it. You have to care about what you're writing. If you don't love what you're writing, do something else.

JIM KOUF *(Rush Hour)*

Having a real life is important to being any kind of writer. Don't just sit behind a desk all day long. You have to live a full life so you have things to write about that are important to you. I have a ranch. I love the outdoors. I hike. I collect art. I've always been into photography. I have four kids. Everything feeds into the work. If your life is empty, then you don't have anything to write about.

SCOTT ROSENBERG *(Con Air)*

Don't write what you know, but write what you know emotionally. You have to be able to share the hopes, dreams and emotions of your characters.

ED SOLOMON *(Men in Black)*

I think everybody enters into writing in different ways and everyone writes differently. Any process of writing is valid if it's done well and invalid if it's done poorly. You have to dig into yourself. You need to have a voice. You need to be original. You have to push yourself. You have to tell a story.

TRAIN YOUR MIND
TO THINK BIG

*"I need to believe something
extraordinary is possible."*
—A Beautiful Mind

One of the biggest challenges for writers is that they are
largely self-trained. That's different from other professionals, like a lawyer or doctor, where the training is straight-forward and structured. In other professions, you usually study a
specialized curriculum, pass a test, and then you're declared
certified and qualified to do your job.

It's not that way for writers.

For writers, there is no predetermined path. Screenwriters
can take creative writing courses or go to film school to study
screenwriting. But writing is an art-form, like painting or com-
posing music. So while the basic mechanics can be taught to
anyone, the ability to create a true work of art can't.

This doesn't mean, though, that you can rely exclusively on

your raw talent. You can't be a great writer without talent, but there are other skills and abilities you need to have too.

Your mind also has to be up to the job. When you're looking for your big idea, you have to do it with a mind that's knowledgeable and informed about what it is you're trying to do. If your career goal is to create blockbuster stories for millions of people, you can't lock yourself away in your room and ignore the outside world where you and all those millions of people live. You have to stay in touch with the world around you, because that's where your ideas are going to come from.

THE TWO WORLDS OF A WRITER

All successful writers understand the importance of keeping a life-long connection to two different worlds.

The first is the real world we live in.

The second is the world of stories.

THE WORLD WE LIVE IN

You can't write about what you don't know, so all successful writers quickly learn that they need to know about a lot of different things. Writers are a curious bunch. They're insatiable readers, talkers, and intellectual explorers. They know the real world is the "raw material" they're going to use to create their stories. And, while the stories they create are make-believe, they have to be accurate about the subject matter they're dramatically representing.

That's what you have to do, too.

Learn about the world from books, magazines, TV, surfing

the net, travel, meeting people, and living a full life. As a writer, you want to always be up-to-date on two aspects of the world we live in. These two broad areas are also great places to look for your big idea.

How the World Works

Any kind of drama works best when it reveals or illuminates the world around us. It shows the audience how things "really work."

Audiences are always drawn to stories that explain the often mysterious mechanics of life in a way that's helpful and beneficial to their own lives. Also, as said before, when writers create an imaginary world in their stories, it has to be believable.

As an aspiring blockbuster screenwriter, your goal is more specific. In your search for a big idea, use your curiosity to seek out the biggest and most dramatic surprises and revelations you can find. The best blockbuster stories are always about what is unique, startling, and unexpected in the world we live in.

How the World Is Changing

A great place to look for a big idea is out on the cutting-edge of our rapidly changing times.

At this point in history, the world is being constantly chopped-and-diced by a dizzying array of sociological, political, technological, and media-driven forces. Whether it's computers, bio-terrorism, robotics, sex, outer space, or the inner mind, there's always a big idea to be found in those places where reality is becoming even more fantastic and surreal.

As a writer you can use these emerging ideas and events for your stories. Read voraciously, but not only in the mainstream media—also seek out smaller fringe magazines and media sources. The more wide-ranging and adventurous you are, the more material you'll have to work with.

THE WORLD OF STORIES

Writers also have to know about the world of stories, because that's another world they want to be a part of.

Since our earliest ancestors gathered around the very first campfire, sharing stories has been our way of communicating who we are, what we've been through, and what we care about. It doesn't matter if a story is spiritual, lustful, boastful, cautionary, or revolutionary, because what they all have in common is they're an on-going reflection and shared record of our lives and experiences.

More importantly, stories have been the medium in which our deepest hopes, dreams, and fears have been shared. Stories have always been with us, so if you want to create new stories that are powerful and bold, you need to know and understand the traditions of storytelling.

Classic Stories

The best way to educate yourself about storytelling is to see how the best writers that came before you have done it. You should seek out all kinds of stories, because great lessons can be learned from the past. Read plays, novels, and short stories. No matter what kind of movie story you're interested in writing, knowing the classic traditions of a story style or genre is enormously helpful and inspirational.

This is especially important if you're starting out as a screenwriter. You're following in the footsteps of the writers who came before you, so you don't want to duplicate what's already been done. You want to use it to springboard your imagination to a higher creative level. You need to understand the past to create the future.

For instance, if you've never read classic drama (try *Oedipus*

Rex by Sophocles or *Medea* by Euripedes), you may be surprised to learn that it's blockbuster storytelling at it's best. There's incredible tragedy, slapstick comedy, twisted sex, spectacle, wars, murder, and mayhem. These plays, and others like them, combine the blockbuster elements of movies like *American Beauty* and *Saving Private Ryan*. The only difference is that back then they wore togas.

Every aspiring screenwriter interested in understanding the basic building blocks of dramatic storytelling should read *The Poetics* by Aristotle. It's old (fourth century, B.C.), but it works surprisingly well as a great how-to guide on what today is considered blockbuster story structure.

Comic Books (Yes—Comic Books!)

Reading comic books will also sharpen your skills and inspire your search for big ideas. Comic books are closer to big budget movies, and visa versa, than any other medium, because they share the same kind of visual energy and imaginative exuberance. That explains why *Superman*, *Batman*, *The Phantom*, *Spiderman*, *Daredevil*, *The X-Men*, *The League of Extraordinary Gentlemen* and others have made it to the big screen.

The best comic books (try anything by Allan Moore or Frank Miller) are crisp and visually exhilarating stories about outrageous and over-sized characters and conflicts that take the reader on a wild, head-spinning ride from the first page to the last.

Most of all, the best comic books illustrate the dramatic power and punch of using bold visual imagery to tell a story. For the blockbuster screenwriter, this is your story-telling goal—to fill that giant, glowing screen with amazing images and pictures.

Classic (and Not So Classic) Movies

Most important of all, of course, is to watch and study movies, lots of them, all kinds, as many as possible.

You'll never come up with a big idea if you don't know what's already been done by other screenwriters before. To think like a screenwriter, you need to understand the history of movies, because the future of any story form is always based in some way on the past.

For blockbuster screenwriters, watching and studying movies is an absolute necessity. Without it, your creative arsenal is never going to be as strong as it should. Because your goal is to come up with a big idea that's a rousing audience-pleaser, a blockbuster screenwriter has to understand what makes great movies great, the mediocre ones mediocre, and why the bad ones are. . . . BAD!

Scream

"Obviously you don't watch enough movies. This is standard horror movie stuff. *Prom Night* revisited. Billy's got killer printed all over his forehead."

—Scream

The screenwriter Kevin Williamson is a great example of a writer who used his understanding of movie history to create a new blockbuster story. In *Scream*, he found a clever way to re-invent the teen horror movie, a genre that was felt to be overdone and stale.

Williamson knew the audience had become bored with the generic sameness of teen horror movies, so he met this challenge head on. He used his knowledge of the genre to create something new. What he did was make his main characters horror-movie experts, so the smart and twisty plot is always a step ahead of the audience. In the past, teen horror movies had fallen into a rut, so audiences had become bored. But in *Scream*, because the characters in the story know horror movies so well, they never do the standard things that had become clichés. This prevented the audience from feeling superior to the movie, because the characters in the movie were every bit as smart as the audience. It took away the "groan factor"—when the audience can't believe the characters are doing something so obviously stupid. The movie succeeded in re-energizing the teen horror genre with a new story style that thrilled and entertained the audience in a fresh new way.

STORY GENRES

Educating yourself about the world of stories should also include a solid understanding of how different story genres work. A story genre is a label for a story that defines it's content, like a detective story, or a love story.

Blockbuster movies are usually genre movies, so examining genres also provides a great place to look for your big idea.

Genres like "action-adventure" and "romantic comedy" are perennial audience favorites on the big screen. Throughout the history of movies, genre stories have been a mainstay in attracting a broad audience. The key to their popularity is that each genre has it's own special elements and appeal. When the audience goes to see an action-adventure movie, they know what kind of entertainment experience they're going to have. It's the same for a comedy, a horror movie, or any other kind of movie genre.

As a blockbuster screenwriter, you need a thorough understanding of why a specific genre is appealing to an audience and how to deliver that in a new and fresh story. Studying movies is the best way to "figure out" what makes a specific genre work. It's also how you'll get creative inspiration for finding your own big genre idea.

Popular Movie Genres

Following are the most popular movie genres. The movies cited as examples in each genre are also a good starting place if you want to figure out what the special qualities of the genre are. But by no means stop there. Never write a blockbuster genre movie unless you know its traditions and fully understand the genre's unique appeal.

ROMANTIC COMEDY
Some Like It Hot, Annie Hall, Sleepless in Seattle, Pretty Woman

HORROR MOVIE
Exorcist, Night of the Living Dead, Texas Chainsaw Massacre, Nightmare on Elm Street

ACTION ADVENTURE
Journey to the Center of the Earth, Raiders of the Lost Ark, Jurassic Park, Armageddon

THRILLER
Psycho, Fatal Attraction, Seven, Silence of the Lambs

SCIENCE FICTION
The Day the Earth Stood Still, Star Wars, E.T., Terminator

ROAD MOVIE
Easy Rider, Midnight Run, Road Trip, Thelma & Louise

COMEDY SPOOF
Airplane, Spaceballs, Austin Powers, Scary Movie

HISTORICAL DRAMA
Braveheart, Glory, Dances With Wolves, Saving Private Ryan

FANTASY
Willow, Conan the Barbarian, Legend, The Wizard of Oz, Lord of the Rings

COMEDY ADVENTURE
Romancing the Stone, Goonies, Honey I Shrunk The Kids, Spy Kids

Alien

In the movie *Alien*, screenwriter Dan O'Bannon created a visual and visceral stunner of a big idea by combining the genres of horror and science fiction into a movie hybrid that appealed to the audiences of both.

From the horror genre, he used one of it's most primal and enduring elements: the monster. He also borrowed another tried-and-true spooky element: people trapped in a creaky and shadowy haunted house.

O'Bannon's creative twist was transplanting these horror elements into a science-fiction landscape. The monster was a horrific and spectacularly unstoppable alien creature. The shadowy haunted house was a creepy spaceship with a maze of twisting, spooky passageways. Because science fiction is more grounded in what's possible, he was also careful to include scientific explanations and a gritty realistic tone to the story. The final result was a science-fiction movie with authentic horror scares.

Feed Your Head

Fill your mind with as much raw material as possible, so you have a depth of material from which to draw.

Writers must know about the real world they live in. They also have to know about the world of storytelling, so they can perform the creative alchemy needed to take the audience to a place they've never been before.

As a blockbuster screenwriter, your curiosity level has to be as big and bold as the ideas you're looking for. That's your goal. You can lock yourself away in your room when you're working on your screenplay, but never lose your connection to the outside world, because that's where your inspiration and story material is going to come from.

You can never forget what it is you want your mind to do—create something new and extraordinary.

BLOCKBUSTER ADVICE

The Training of a Blockbuster Screenwriter

As said at the beginning of the chapter, there's no one way to train as a writer or as a blockbuster screenwriter. However, there are broad areas of knowledge that you need to educate yourself about, and that's what we've just finished identifying. With screenwriting there's also more specific information about story structure and format that we'll cover later in the book.

You can learn these skills on your own; many writers do. But there's also the option of more formal training. With the increasing popularity of movies, film schools and film programs have grown in popularity as well, and the top film schools have become "the hot ticket" for aspiring movie-makers.

The advantages of going to film school are worth at least some consideration, both for what can be learned and also for help breaking into the business.

As you'll see, the screenwriters cover the spectrum. Several went to the top film schools, while others started out with almost no formal training.

DAVID BENIOFF *(The 25th Hour)*

Most of my training has come from meeting with directors on my screenplays. Spike Lee is directing *The 25th Hour* and David Fincher is directing my screenplay *Stay*. Literally, I've had thirty hours of meetings with Fincher. Half the time we'll be talking about the script and the rest we'll be talking about movies. Hearing David Fincher talk about Alfred Hitchcock is a great education.

I think a lot of screenwriters don't read as much as they should. I know a lot of screenwriters who've never read *Casablanca*, which to me is kind of shocking. It would be like a novelist who never read *The Great Gatsby*. You've got to be aware of what came before and what's worked before. I think you have to have a passion for the form. Before I started writing my first screenplay, I was able to get the screenplays to my ten all-time favorite movies and read them.

NEAL BRENNAN *(Half Baked)*

I ended up getting into NYU film school after high school. I wasn't a very good student, and I'm still not sure why I got in. When I got there I remember being really intimidated by the other kids, because they were all so pretentious and seemed so erudite. They'd all watched *Wings of Desire* ad nauseum.

So basically, during my first year, I started spending time at comedy clubs in the Village, hanging out and basically working for free. I also befriended Dave Chappelle, who was my age and a comedian, and Jay Mohr, another comedian. I was having more fun hanging out with them writing jokes than I was in school, so I dropped out of NYU.

I was eighteen. I started writing a screenplay with another comedian. I'd read some screenplays and some TV scripts through connections at the comedy clubs, but no books. Nothing happened with the script. I was also writing a lot of comedy sketches. There was a show on MTV called *Comickaze* that I wrote for.

But this wasn't a good period. I was really poor, close to destitute. I was twenty pounds lighter, smoking cigarettes. I was officially a ragamuffin, one of those kids you see hanging out in

Washington Square Park. But writing comedy sketches is great training. You're learning character, voice, and scene structure.

I ended up interning on the MTV show *Singled Out*. When the two writers on the show quit, I was promoted. I ended up being the only writer. And that's my best advice about getting a job. If you want to work somewhere, just go there and work for free.

PHILIP EISNER *(Event Horizon)*

I've never taken a screenwriting course. I went to Stanford and they didn't have any. But they do have a very strong creative writing program in the English department. I took *Short Story I* and *Short Story II*, and those were probably the best training I could have had. The most important thing is to develop a sense of what's good writing and what's bad writing.

If you're not going to write without pressure and a deadline, then maybe you should go to film school. It really depends on whether you need the structure or not. At the same time, if you're not going to write without outside pressure, then you're not a writer and you shouldn't do it.

In terms of going to film school just to network and have it on your resume, I also believe it's all about the script. If your script is crap, it doesn't matter if you went to the best film school in the country and you're Jerry Bruckheimer's best friend. A crappy screenplay is a crappy screenplay.

AKIVA GOLDSMAN *(A Beautiful Mind)*

The myth about me is that I sold my first screenplay and it's true. But I had also worked very hard as a fiction writer for ten years and that's how I learned the craft of telling stories.

When I first started to consider screenwriting, I took Robert McKee's course. I'm a big advocate of McKee. What I learned, and I say it with great gratitude, is structure. Fiction writing is sort of mercurial and mysterious. But screenplays, at least anatomically, are predictable. They have a clearer structure that can be learned.

I think you also need to read and write constantly in order to be a good writer. Whether you do it in a formal program or not varies according to the individual. What's important is the need to read screenplays to understand the literal grammar. But most of all, what you need to learn is narrative, how to tell a story.

DAVID GOYER *(Blade)*

I went to undergraduate film school at USC. One of the things that going to a big film school instills in you is it prepares you for how competitive this business can be. Unfortunately, a lot of times it's not just about being talented, it's also about how well you can sell yourself and promote yourself and not get discouraged. Because a big part of getting noticed as a screenwriter is getting your foot in the door and conveying a certain level of confidence.

Nowadays, I don't think going to film school is important at all, but if you have the opportunity, it doesn't hurt either. It's easy to get the training you need without film school. Go on the Internet and download screenplays and take a couple of courses. I've read some pretty great screenplays that came from people who had no formal training and horrible screenplays from people that had the film school stamp of approval. It's all about the talent of the writer. There's so much you can pick up without going to a film school.

DAVID HAYTER *(X-Men)*

I've read all the books, Syd Field and all the others. But my training was really working with Bryan Singer for 13 months on *X-Men*. I had a certain flair for writing and an understanding of character from an acting perspective. But Bryan really whipped it into shape and taught me the basics of A-list filmmaking.

Formal training can give you a lot of the tools you need, but in another way it can leave you completely unprepared for the realities of constructing a film for a studio and the realities of business strategy. Working with a director is invaluable. It's like the difference between painting by numbers and real painting.

You're calling on parts of your creative self that haven't been necessarily touched on in formal academic situations.

The best advice I can give is something I read in an interview with Woody Allen. He said, if you want to make movies, watch movies. And really try to understand why all the creative decisions were made. Why the director shot a scene in a certain way. Why the screenwriter chose to structure something a certain way.

I try to watch a great film every night. I'll watch films again and again to understand how they work. Once you can open that door in your head and really study great films, that to me is far more valuable than anything you'll get in an academic situation.

JIM KOUF *(Rush Hour)*

In college, I was an English major, and I started writing plays. I really enjoyed writing dialogue. And I kept getting really good grades on everything I wrote. So I just started to think, this is something I'm really good at.

When I decided to be a screenwriter, I educated myself by reading a bunch of scripts. That taught me what movie stories were and how they're written. I wrote a couple of spec TV scripts and that got me an agent.

If I was starting out today, I'd go to film school. It's important mostly because you make friends with people who become a part of the industry, too. So much about working in the business is knowing people, and that would be a good start. Plus it will give you an understanding of the different elements in making a movie.

But also see movies. Beginning screenwriters really need to know the history of movies. They need to see the classic movies like *The Third Man* and *Lawrence of Arabia* and *To Kill A Mockingbird*. It's silly to say you want to be a screenwriter and not to have seen the great classic movies that are the history of the field you want work in.

DALE LAUNER *(My Cousin Vinny)*

I started out wanting to be a filmmaker. Back then, everything

I read said the primary vision came from the director. So I decided to be a director. I went to Cal State Northridge and started making films in the film department. After looking at the results, I started to have a greater appreciation of the writing than the directing.

ANDREW MARLOWE *(Air Force One)*

I got an MFA from USC'S graduate screenwriting program. I think a formal screenwriting education can save you a lot of time, depending on the program. Nobody can teach you how to write well. There's a certain instinct to creating the cinematic or dramatic moment. There's a certain instinct in terms of controlling the audience.

But having the craft to be able to express that in its most effective terms will come either from you being a genius, finding it out through trial-and-error, or somebody giving you some parameters to operate in. So for me, formal screenwriting training was enormously helpful.

What training can do for you is put you in a community with people who share your same interests. It will give you a sophisticated audience that can give you specific feedback in a language you can understand. Because after going through a series of screenwriting courses, you all speak the same language.

SCOTT ROSENBERG *(Con Air)*

I had been in Los Angeles for about two years when I decided that instead of just being a bartender, I'd be a bartender who was going to one of the hotshot film schools. I was feeling that the one thing you lose in LA is your individuality, because everybody is writing a screenplay. So why not be a screenwriter who's going to film school? I was at USC for about a year, then I transferred to UCLA.

Film school can be good for two reasons. First, it makes you write, and you're constantly getting feedback from your peers. Plus, I had to make films. I hated it, but at least you learn the technical process.

A friend of mine was doing his thesis film at USC, and I wrote it for him. It got a lot of great buzz. Joel Silver saw it and loved it. He said pitch me whatever you want. So we pitched him something and he bought it. I quickly got two more writing jobs. Joel hired us to do two *Tales from the Crypt* episodes. So I was off and running.

I think it's also important to read. I read a lot of contemporary novels. When I want to be humbled and inspired I read Philip Roth and he blows me away. The same with Martin Amis and Don DeLillo. I don't read a lot of scripts. I watch a lot of old movies. I'm dating an actress and we watch movies together. We have Billy Wilder night once a week. We're going through all his movies. After that, we're going to start John Huston night.

ED SOLOMON *(Men In Black)*

I took some playwriting courses at UCLA, but I've never taken a screenwriting course. I was actually an Economics major. When I first started out, I read a couple of screenwriting books, but I can't remember which ones. As recently as last year I took a fiction writing class, which I've been doing on and off for the last few years. But everything can be helpful. Talking to writers, reading the books, watching movies. Going to film school is good because you're surrounded by people trying to do similar things. Especially for people in their formative years, the twenties and thirties. When you're in an environment where everybody's excited, enthusiastic and competitive with each other, it can be helpful. But it can also really screw people up and make them quit forever. It depends on your personality.

I didn't go to film school, but that was my path.

IMAGINATION IS YOUR BIGGEST CREATIVE TOOL

"Rocky, after this you'll be eating thunder and shitting lightening."

—Rocky

Now we come to the final creative aspect you need to nurture as a blockbuster screenwriter, your *imagination*. You use your imagination to blast what's in your heart and mind far beyond what you ever dreamed possible, because if you don't, then your story writing abilities will be confined to your everyday experiences—and that's never enough to deserve a place on a movie screen.

After all, movies are an escape from real life. The best ones not only make escape possible, they also have the ability to exhilarate the audience with thrills, chills, surprises, and plot twists, all leading up to an edge-of-your-seat, super-charged-ending. Blockbuster movies deliver sights and sensations that are bigger, bolder, and better than normal life.

The way movies do that is through the imagination of the writer. Imagination is the ability to take what you know and transform it into something that transcends normal life.

UNLEASH YOUR IMAGINATION

Learning to use your imagination to it's fullest is probably the biggest part of being a blockbuster screenwriter. The first step to doing this is asking questions as you go about your everyday life. It's an inner dialogue writers have with themselves. Maybe you see an interesting person that strikes your curiosity, or you read a surprising article in a magazine.

Keep Asking Yourself Questions

Writers start by asking questions to launch their imaginations on an inner journey in search of the unexpected and unique. Questions like:

Why?
How?
Why not?
What would happen if?

This process can provide the keys to opening the locked doors in your mind that lead to the magical and creative places in your imagination. As a blockbuster screenwriter, you need to keep opening these doors until you reach that place in your imagination that's filled with spectacular and original ideas. The goal is to explore the deep labyrinth of your imagination until you come up with a big idea you can turn into a great movie that appeals to a broad audience.

The following is a great example of a screenwriter who combined his industry instincts with his imagination, to write, not just a million dollar screenplay, but a $3 million dollar screenplay.

FROM IDEA
TO MILLION
DOLLAR $ALE
Dale Launer

A friend of mine once told me that when a new studio is formed, the first thing they do is go out and buy a screenplay for a lot of money. They do it to signal to the agencies that they have money and they're open for business. Then the agencies will start sending all their A-list material.

This is also the time when Jeffrey Katzenberg was fired from Disney and formed DreamWorks with David Geffen and Steven Spielberg.

I said to myself, I'm going to write a screenplay that Spielberg would like, a big sci-fi action movie. I really pushed my imagination to come up with something different. I came up with an idea about a guy who goes to a psychiatrist because he thinks he's a monster. It turns out, he is. I always liked movies that started small, then went off in a different direction and got bigger and bigger. So this was going to be a movie about a monster that gets bigger and bigger. I also wanted it to be both scary and funny.

I wrote it while staying at a hotel in New York on vacation with my girlfriend. I stayed for another week after she went back home. Most of it I wrote that week, then I went back to Los Angeles and finished it.

If your script deals with a certain kind of material, it's always best to go out with it when something else in that genre has been a big hit. I knew I needed a big, expensive effects movie that had some humor in it. I decided to send my script out in the fall, to capitalize on the success of *Men in Black*.

Although I've never had an agent before, I knew I needed one for this project. I went to a friend who had just become a new agent at CAA [Creative Artists Agency], Jim Lefkowitz. During a meeting with Steven Spielberg, the head of CAA gives him my script to read. He read it overnight, loved it, and called Katzenberg the next day.

Katzenberg calls Lefkowitz and says, "We want to buy this script. We'll give you $3 million for it, but you have to decide in fifteen minutes." Lefkowitz calls me immediately and tells me the offer. I can hear trembling in his voice. I know he's nervous because I've got a reputation as a maverick. He's afraid that I'm not going to do it.

He's right. I tell him to ask for more time and more money. We ended up getting more time, but not more money.

We made the deal for $3 million. The script is called *Bad Dog*. The bad news is the movie has never been made. The good news is they don't make you give the money back.

THINK OUTSIDE THE BOX

As a blockbuster screenwriter, you have to always be original and think "outside the box."

When you're pushing your imagination to come up with a big idea, use the following techniques and suggestions to stimulate bigger and imaginative new ways of thinking.

Break Away From The Usual Story Conventions

Look at different kinds of stories and think about how they're normally told. You'll notice story techniques that never change. If a technique worked well once, everyone copies it until the next new idea comes along. It's up to you to imagine and invent that new technique.

Imagine what would happen if you completely changed some of the usual elements, or tell the story from a different point of view, or bring in unexpected new elements.

By doing this you can re-energize a story that's been overdone and make it fresh again. Blockbuster screenwriting means mixing story ideas that are unexpected with those that have proven themselves to be successful.

This is what James Cameron did in *True Lies*. He conceived a new kind of spy movie by veering away from the martini-sipping playboy prototype of James Bond. Instead, his lead character,

Arnold Schwarzenegger, is an international spy not only fighting vicious bad guys, but also married and saddled with the same everyday problems as any other weary dad. At home, he's just an average Joe, trying his best to hold his own against a rebellious teenager and an independent wife. Away from home though, it's a different story, because he's a larger-than-life hero battling to save the world. With this imaginative twist, Cameron breathes new life into an otherwise tired story line.

Beetlejuice

Screenwriters Michael McDowell and Warren Skareen put an original twist in their script for the haunted-house movie *Beetlejuice*.

Traditionally, in this type of story, it's the humans who are desperately trying to get rid of the ghosts. But in *Beetlejuice*, the main characters are a young couple living in the country, who are killed in a car accident, and have now become ghosts. In this case, the story is about how these two likeable ghosts desperately try to get rid of an obnoxious family from New York City who move into their house. The still very pleasant looking ghosts are the sympathetic heroes and the humans are the villains, a complete flip-flop on the way the story had always been told.

The two ghosts, played by Alec Baldwin and Geena Davis, do everything in their supernatural power to scare the family away, but it's a losing battle. The screenwriters also used a lot of off-the-wall humor, instead of going for the usual ghost story scares, like the invention of the title character, *Beetlejuice*, a lunatic, wise-cracking, slime-ball ghost.

What resulted was a wonderfully quirky and entertaining movie, because the screenwriters broke through the normal expectations of how a ghost story has to be told.

Invent A New World

Make-believe landscapes are key elements in the collective worlds of fairy tales, myths, and legends, as well as the futuristic world of science fiction and the primal, dark world of horror.

We've always conjured up imaginary beings and stories that personify our deepest dreams and nightmares. The trick here is to be original and conjure up your own variation on ghosts, angels, monsters, dragons, vampires, outer-space aliens, and countless other make-believe creatures and creations.

Look in your own imagination for great new stories that use these mythic archetypes. Big screen audiences love new twists on the imaginary creatures they grew up with. For example, in *Gremlins*, the screenwriter Chris Columbus used a mythic creature, the gremlin, to write a movie that was free-wheeling, fast-paced, and fun. The bad gremlins were bratty wicked fur balls that wreaked mayhem and havoc with gleeful delight. Even though gremlins are well-known mythic creatures, the way Columbus re-imagined them was fresh, entertaining, and unexpected. Audiences responded accordingly, making *Gremlins* the fourth-highest grossing film of 1984.

Likewise, Stephen Sommers's screenplay for *The Mummy* performed a similar re-imagining of a familiar fantasy monster. In previous movies, the mummy had been a lumbering and silent creature with about as much personality as a pile of dirty sheets. Sommers discarded this boring concept and created a mummy that was a vengeful terminator with almost invincible supernatural powers.

Here was a memorable mummy that could run circles around all the other stumbling mummies that came before. Once again, movie-goers reacted positively to the change by making *The Mummy* one of the top grossing movies of 1999.

Kick the Story Up Another Notch

You can also use your imagination to make any kind of story more intense, mysterious, outrageous, heartwarming, or surprising than anything that's been done before. Whatever is the current outer limit for the kind of story you want to write, imagine a way that breaks through that with bigger imagination and style.

When *Airplane* came out, it was a huge success, because it pushed the comedy envelope with a smarter and more uninhibited go-for-the-joke tone than what had come before. For the audience, it gave them even more of what they wanted from a movie comedy. It had a good story, but more importantly, the comic tone was relentlessly funny and outrageous, delivering non-stop laughs.

The Road Warrior, a hardcore futuristic action movie, kicked it up another notch, too. When it came out in 1981, it raised the bar on big-screen movie action. It was raw and exciting, filled with exhilarating crash-and-burn car chases, visually extreme characters, and brutal violence. The movie's action was more fast-paced, explosive and intense than what had been done before, and it's still the stylistic inspiration for many of the high-octane action movies that have followed.

Answer Big Questions With a Big Idea

Mysteries and questions that have dogged the human race since the beginning of time can be a great inspiration for your big idea. Movies that answer these big questions have also proven to be audience favorites.

Blockbuster movies have taken on such age-old questions as: What's reality?—*The Matrix*. Is there life after death?—*Flatliners*. Are we alone in the universe?—*Independence Day*.

Put your imagination to work and come up with your own version of a big idea that answers a big question.

Take the Audience to Forbidden Places

Audiences love to see what they're not supposed to see. People are fascinated with the secret, forbidden, strange, and extraordinary. They're tantalized by anything that's off-limits and taboo.

Like when the screenwriter Mark Protosevich took us inside the mind of a serial killer in *The Cell*, visually revealing its dark secrets and psychological terrors. Or when James Cameron took us down into the hidden depths of the ocean in *The Abyss*, and the audience experienced both it's surreal beauty and it's awesome, unexpected dangers.

Look for a big idea that takes the audience behind-the-scenes to a secret and taboo place that's never been revealed before.

Push Your Characters to Extremes

Look for story landscapes where your characters can be tested and challenged to the absolute, gut-bursting limits of their physical, emotional, and psychological endurance, then push them some more. Audiences love to vicariously identify with characters in extreme mind-and-body-stressing situations. They identify with a character that has the odds stacked against them. The more vividly the character is portrayed as an under-dog, the more satisfying the final victory if it comes.

Screenwriter William Broyles used this technique in *Cast Away*. The character Tom Hanks played tested his resources to their limits as he struggled to survive on a deserted island. It was a grueling physical and psychological challenge that demanded every last drop of his outer strength and inner spirit.

In the *Rocky* movies, Sylvester Stallone, who was both the star and the screenwriter, always created larger-than-life opponents that demanded the absolute best from Rocky if he wanted to win. Rocky is always the underdog going into battle with an opponent who seems far superior—which, of course, makes his surprising victory even more amazing and satisfying.

Find a Love Story with a New Twist

Love is our most powerful, mysterious, and intensely human emotion. It's also a major element in most movies. Coming up with a new way to tell a great love story is always a big idea. Even in the wildest blow-it-up, shoot-em-up blockbuster movies, there's almost always a love story at the center of it all. Romantic comedies, too, are one of the most popular and enduring movie genres. *Tootsie, Pretty Woman,* and *What Women Want* were all clever and funny romantic comedies, in which the screenwriters found an imaginative new way to tell the story of two unlikely people falling in love.

If you can find a smart new way to tell a great love story, it's a winning idea for blockbuster success.

What Dreams May Come

In *What Dreams May Come*, the screenwriter Ron Bass wrote a powerful love story about a husband separated from his wife and children by death.

Robin Williams plays the husband, whose love for his wife is so strong, he literally journeys to the depths of Hell to be with her. His macabre and horrific trip through Hell is a visually stunning quest that takes the audience to the ultimate forbidden place. In order to write this story, Bass clearly searched the depths of his own imagination to create a visual tour-de-force that dramatizes the incredible pain of losing somebody you love. The movie is emotionally painful, but it's also a deeply beautiful love story—because, in the end, love conquers all.

Create Something Cool

Cool is hard to define.

That said, blockbuster movies are almost always cool. They're usually about outsiders breaking in, or insiders breaking out, with all sorts of fun-to-watch, high-energy exploits. Generally, cool stories are socially wild, culturally rebellious, and showcase a way of life that's an adolescent fantasy come true. Here's a rule about cool you can use: Whatever teenagers are obsessed with is always a good place to let your imagination loose. If you're clueless about all this, it's another reason you should be wide-ranging in your media interests, because it can show you what's cool.

Vin Diesel is cool in *XXX*. *Ocean's 11*, the original and the remake, are cool. Action is cool. Monsters are cool. True love is cool. Thelma and Louise are super-cool. *The Rocky Horror Picture Show* will always be cool. *Cool Hand Luke* is still cool.

Try it.

Break the Normal Rules of Narrative Structure

Forget what you learned in high school and look for creative and offbeat narrative structures that break the rules. You can intrigue and totally captivate an audience if you completely startle their expectations. Think about how you felt the first time you saw *The Usual Suspects*, *Pulp Fiction*, *Fight Club*, and *Memento*. These movies all used quirky plot structures and story techniques to great effect. Each played with traditional narrative organization in a different way, but all of them took the audience on a new kind of movie ride that was exciting and memorable.

If this is a direction you want to pursue, just remember it's difficult to do well, which is why the successful ones are so unique and noteworthy.

Go Where No Writer has Gone Before

The goal here is to use your imagination and creativity to be groundbreaking and radically new. Be a story-telling explorer who discovers a big idea that's so different it's beyond the scope of anything that's been done before.

Imagine an idea that's been completely unimaginable until you created it.

PART TWO

WHAT YOU NEED TO KNOW ABOUT THE AUDIENCE

WRITING FOR
A BIG AUDIENCE

If there's one secret mantra that every blockbuster screenwriter lives by it's this:

I'M WRITING A STORY FOR A BIG AUDIENCE

With the possible exception of television, there's no other form of writing where the size of the audience is such an important objective in the creative process.

As a blockbuster screenwriter, you're creating a story that has to hook as big an audience as possible, because that's what you're getting paid for. It's part of the job description.

Blockbuster screenwriters are paid the big bucks because they know how to construct a story that will bring millions of people to the movie theater and entertain them when they get there. Which means you have to develop an understanding of what movie audiences want when they buy a ticket and start munching their popcorn.

What's the mystical appeal and attraction of going to the movies?

Movies are called an escape and it's true.

When people go to the movies, they want to leave their everyday lives behind and be whisked off to a place that's faraway from all their countless nagging worries. But audiences don't go to movies to escape their emotions. In fact, the opposite is true. Audiences go to movies to have their emotions stimulated.

BLOCKBUSTER MOVIES ARE INTENSE

No matter what kind of story you're writing, audiences expect blockbuster movies to be bigger and better in every way possible.

They want to be hooked at the very beginning, then have an entertainment experience that's super-intense. If it's a love story, they want it to be the grandest, most intense love story ever. If it's a horror movie, they want it to be the scariest, most terrifying horror movie ever. Blockbuster movies always aspire to be a movie-experience homerun, never just a double or triple.

Speed

In the movie *Speed*, the screenwriter Graham Yost came up with an innovative idea for a maximum intensity action story that had audiences on the edge of their seat for most of the movie. Keanu Reeves is a cop who has to save the passengers on an L.A. bus that's rigged to blow up if the speedometer drops below 50 MPH.

The tension is non-stop as the audience watches the bus careen wildly through crowded city streets with the bomb always on the verge of exploding. The fact that innocent people are a split-second away from being blown to smithereens makes for a heart-pounding ride for all who watch this scary, exciting, and ultimately triumphant film.

Audiences go to movies to be entertained, but that's only part of it. We're all different, so we're all entertained by different kinds of stories. But there's one test that all movies have to pass to connect with an audience.

It's the most important element in any story, and it's what all blockbuster screenwriters strive for.

AUDIENCES WANT TO BE EMOTIONALLY CHARGED

Most people's lives are messy and uncontrollable.

Audiences go to blockbuster movies because they know they'll feel emotions in a vivid and freeing way. They'll feel joy, happiness, fear, excitement, and sadness. For those two hours, they'll experience the intense emotions of life from the safety of their theater seat. As said, audiences go to movies to escape their own lives, but they also go to feel *more alive*. When you go to a great movie, you're able to experience the depth and range of human emotions through the characters in the story.

A blockbuster movie is able to connect with the heart of the audience in a powerful way.

Try it yourself. Think about your favorite movies. Now think about why you like them so much.

It's because of a feeling they gave you, isn't it? Your favorite movies, even now, make you feel an emotion. You were sitting in the audience and a story came to life on that giant, glowing screen that made you feel something so intensely it's still a part of you. It made you laugh out loud, cry real tears, be goose-bumpy and scared, or wide-eyed with excitement.

Most likely, what you remember isn't so much the plot as how the story made you feel while watching it. What happened was something that's almost mystical. You were sitting in a dark theater and you became a part of the story. What was happening to the characters was also happening to you. You felt emotions that were as real as real life.

And those emotions were big.

That's what a blockbuster movie does.

And that's the creative challenge. You want to create stories that will touch an audience in a very intense and thrilling way. You want an audience to scream, cheer and be completely connected to the story. You want them on the edge of their seats, or with their hands over their eyes, or reaching for a tissue to wipe away tears.

THE MIND AND IMAGINATION ARE GOOD, TOO

Audiences want to feel an emotional connection more than anything else. It's the most powerful and satisfying feeling a movie can give them.

But audiences also enjoy stories that appeal to the mind and imagination.

Mysteries and non-realistic stories (fantasy, science fiction) fall into this category.

At the center of a mystery is an intellectual puzzle. The audience, identifying with the main character, is entertained by the challenge of solving the puzzle. The audience enjoys the intellectual obstacle course of trying to figure out the mystery.

In blockbuster movies, the bigger and more challenging the mystery, the better. A mystery is always a good story structure, because it hooks the audience right away. In blockbuster movies you want to create a mystery that can fill the big screen with a story that's exuberantly entertaining and visually distinctive.

Stay is a psychological thriller about a university psychologist who's desperately trying to stop a student from committing suicide. The mind-twisting narrative piles mystery on top of mystery as the psychologist is gradually pulled into the boy's troubled and horrific world, where reality itself may be in question.

FROM IDEA
TO MILLION
DOLLAR $ALE
David Benioff

Stay was my second script after *The 25th Hour*. My agents and I thought the script would sell, but not for a lot of money. They sent it to twenty producers. It was such a bizarre day. I was sitting around waiting for a call and nothing was happening. Then my agent finally called and said five different studios wanted it and a bidding war had started. The price was already over a million.

I just remember lying down on the floor of my apartment. I couldn't even comprehend it. I was hyper-ventilating. It was the weirdest thing. You know intellectually it's good news, but your body is so over-the-top, you don't know how to deal with it. My adrenaline was pumping. I was sweating. It almost feels like it's bad news because of the reaction. I was so hyper I wanted to go to the gym, but my agent wouldn't let me leave the apartment.

The deal was finally closed at 8:30 that night for $1.8 million. When it sold, my parents couldn't even talk. There was an article in *Variety*, and I faxed it to my dad's office.

Fantasy and science fiction stories give the audience a feeling of wonder and amazement that's also entertaining.

The big screen is a great place for these kinds of stories, because they're told with images that are stunning and unexpected. Strange and bizarre sights glow in the theater. Fantastic landscapes and creatures are revealed. They come from another world, or from another reality. The audience's imagination is pushed and stretched in an exciting new way.

What's always most important, though, is the emotional connection an audience feels with a story. Even with stories that are appealing to the mind and imagination, there has to be a strong emotional element for the audience to be fully connected to the movie.

Armageddon

Armageddon illustrates how a movie that appeals to the audience's imagination is made stronger by also touching the heart.

The film is a super-macho science-fiction movie with action and explosions galore. While it's lots of fun and visually spectacular, the emotional heart of the movie is the relationship between the main character, played by Bruce Willis, and his daughter, played by Liv Tyler.

In the story, Willis leads a scruffy team of misfits into space to save Earth from a gigantic-planet-threatening meteor. At the end, he sacrifices his life to save the world, and in doing so, the audience feels the pain of losing somebody you love through the eyes of a daughter.

While the bombastic thrills and excitement are a key to the movie's appeal, it's the love between Willis and his daughter that touches the audience the most.

Without this relationship at the center of the story, the movie would have been just a big-screen fireworks extravaganza without an emotional core for the audience to connect with.

OTHER AUDIENCE CONSIDERATIONS

Following are other broad qualities to consider when developing your movie idea. The movie audience is not a uniform mass with only one opinion, which is why there are so many different kinds of movies. But there are several general characteristics that many blockbuster movies share.

Blockbuster Movies Appeal to Kids

Kids are the biggest movie-going audience segment, so they're directly responsible for the success of most blockbuster movies. Almost all the top-grossing movies (see the list in chapter 18) are unabashed kid-flicks that also appeal to adults. They're all fun, exciting and relentlessly entertaining.

The stories are also about basic values that kids can understand. Fighting for what's right. Helping friends. Being strong and courageous against overwhelming odds.

What makes the story extra-fun, of course, is that the movie characters are doing all this as they blast through outer space, or flee the crunching jaws of a stampeding dinosaur.

Blockbuster Movies Are for Adults, Too

But adults also love movies, so it's always a great opportunity for a smart screenwriter to write a blockbuster story for them as well. *Titanic* and *Forest Gump* are examples of hit movies that appealed directly to adults.

While both have great spectacle and scope, and they're very much about important human values, they're also more adult in tone, without the abundance of kid-friendly thrills and chills.

The Story Speaks to Our Times

One of the reasons *Titanic* and *Forrest Gump* were popular with older audiences is because they dramatized something important about the national mood and character.

Both were heart-tugging mythic love stories, but they were also stories about who we are as a country. They explored the innocence, the courage, the hope, and also the murky and often brutal dark-side of the American soul.

Big Roles for Big Stars

It's always a great idea to write a screenplay that has a terrific role for a movie star. Movie stars, after all, are created when audiences vote their approval by going to see their movies. If this is a creative route you want to pursue, just be sure you do your homework first and understand the kind of roles a star is best at.

Harrison Ford does one kind of movie role wonderfully, while Jim Carrey is best in a completely different kind of story. The same is true for Julia Roberts, Sandra Bullock and Meg Ryan. (In chapter 9, Andrew Marlowe explains how he came up with a story idea tailor-made for Arnold Schwarzenegger that became a hit movie.)

Audiences Love Genre Movies

As said in chapter 4, genre movies are appealing to audiences because they know what kind of entertainment ride they're going to have.

More specifically, a movie genre identifies the emotions an audience will feel during the movie. In fact, audiences will chose a genre because they want a specific emotional experience.

People go to comedies because they know they'll laugh and have fun. They go to horror movies to feel the vicarious exhilaration of being scared and in danger.

Dramas will touch the heart. Romantic comedies will be funny, but they'll also be heartwarming and joyful when the couple finally comes together at the end.

As a blockbuster screenwriter, you want to touch an audience's heart and thrill their minds and imaginations, because that's what every movie-goer wants when the lights go down and the movie begins.

Writing For
An Audience

Successful screenwriters become who they are because they understand the goal of creating movie stories audiences will love. All dramatic writing has to come from a personal place, but blockbuster movies have to appeal to as many people as possible. They're written for a big audience by screenwriters who have the talent and skill to fill thousands and thousands of movie theaters with the stories they create.

DAVID GOYER *(Blade)*

I think if you're writing mainstream Hollywood movies, you have to have an awareness of the audience. I think you have to be aware of audience expectations in terms of what has come before.

You have to understand genre. You have to understand how your movie will be sold. A lot of times when I'm writing a script, I'll think about what the trailer for this movie would be. There are often lines I will put in my scripts and I'll have a bet with the director it will be in the trailer.

ANDREW MARLOWE *(Air Force One)*

You have to write for an audience. If you're going to be contemptuous of the audience and say, "I'm not writing for the masses," then why should someone with $60 million invest in your vision? These people have to recoup their investment, or at least have a chance of recouping their investment.

THE AUDIENCE LOVES HEROES

*"Without pain, without sacrifice,
we wouldn't have nothing."*
—Fight Club

The best way to connect with an audience is with your main character or hero, because it's through this character that the audience experiences the story.

It's absolutely essential that the audience identify in some way with your main character, or your story will not be a blockbuster movie. Blockbuster movies have main characters that embody a mixture of strengths an audience will be attracted to and weaknesses they can relate to.

The objective is to involve the audience as active participants in the action and not allow them to be passive observers. You want the audience to be psychologically and emotionally "in the story." This happens most effectively when they strongly identify with your main character.

Think about your favorite movies, how you felt during every punch, slap, kiss, car crash, act of courage, double-cross, and emotion, painful or otherwise, the main character experienced. This is what happens with the best movies. The main characters remain etched in our minds forever.

CREATING A BLOCKBUSTER MAIN CHARACTER

There are several key traits that make for a memorable main character. In blockbuster movies, of course, you want characters to be as vivid and dramatic as possible. Following are the broad traits for constructing a main character that's strong and memorable.

The Main Character Has to Want Something

Every great main character must want something in the story. More specifically, there are two types of dramatic wants that need to be developed: a physical want and an emotional want. Both are necessary for creating a main character that is complex enough to both drive the action of the story and also be emotionally interesting to the audience.

A PHYSICAL WANT This is your character's goal in the story. This goal can be as varied as finding an insane serial killer (Jodie Foster in *Silence of the Lambs*), helping a young, emotionally disturbed boy (Bruce Willis in *The Sixth Sense*), or ruining Christmas in Whoville (Jim Carrey in *How the Grinch Stole Christmas*).

Countering this goal, there must also be a force of opposition. This is called "the conflict." The conflict can be a tornado, a swarm of killer bees, a psychotic madman, an outer-space alien, or anything else that stands in the way of your main characters getting what they want.

This simple dynamic of two opposing forces is what drives the plot. It sets up "the basic dramatic question." *Is the main character going to win, or is the conflict going to win?* The intensity of the audience's support for the main character, and their interest in the character's fate, keeps them engaged in every twist and turn as the story unfolds.

AN EMOTIONAL WANT This want is an aspect of the main character's psychological or spiritual world. The main character might not even be aware of this inner want, but it's what the story is about on the deepest personal level.

The main character wants to belong, be accepted, be loved, be better, smarter, happier, or wiser in some fundamental way. This want is like a missing piece of their inner emotional puzzle that's prevented the character from being the best they can be.

This want can be varied too. In *Silence of the Lambs*, Jodie Foster secretly wants to stop being haunted by nightmares from her childhood. In *The Sixth Sense*, Bruce Willis wants to heal the wrenching guilt he feels from not being able to help one his patients. In *How the Grinch Stole Christmas*, Jim Carrey, as the Grinch, is miserable because, way down deep, he wants to stop being a grouchy loner and experience the Christmas joy of giving to others.

While the battle with the conflict drives the plot, it also gives the main character an opportunity to fulfill this inner want. That's what the extraordinary challenges in the story bring about. As the main character confronts the conflict on a physical level, he or she also has to call on inner resources. If the story has a happy ending, a large part of that happiness comes from the main character having his or her inner emotional want fulfilled.

The Matrix

In *The Matrix*, the Wachowski brothers wrote one of the all-time great blockbuster movies. It had everything—a troubled main character, spectacular action, lots of guns, great escapes, mind-bending twists and turns, a love story, brain teasing philosophical mysteries, and a whole world that kept mutating and morphing like a sixties flashback.

It was mythic and fast and cosmically cool. It was also a metaphoric coming-of-age story, an origin-of-the-hero story, and a save-the-world story, with high-energy elements borrowed from some of the best blockbuster comic books, movies, and media stuff in the culture.

Keanu Reeves plays the main character, Neo. The conflicts were vivid and intense. Neo fights for his life against an overwhelmingly powerful enemy that wants nothing less than the enslavement of everything he cares for. Neo's physical want in the story is to stay alive and save the world.

But the underlying heart of the story is emotional. Neo is seeking answers to important personal questions. *Who am I? What's my destiny? What's my purpose in life?* Along with the non-stop action and visual pyrotechnics, the movie is also about a character struggling with life-defining issues and mysteries. And it is this inner want that gives the movie its strong emotional appeal.

Identifying what your main character wants in the story is a fundamental step in creating a character the audience will be captivated by and identify with. Having both a physical and an emotional want is essential. Also, for both, make sure "the want" is important. The physical want should be big enough to insure that your main character is the centerpiece of the story. The emotional want should be important enough so that it will change the character's life if it's fulfilled.

Your Main Character Must Be Unique

Exactly who your main character is going to be has a lot to do with the kind of story you're writing. You might need a scientist, a cheerleader, a female business executive, or even a fish, as in *Finding Nemo*.

But no matter what kind of main character you create for your story, human or otherwise, this character has to be special in some way. That is, the character has to possess a quality that sets him or her apart from everyone else in the story.

It's not the job, sex, or age that audiences connect with. The audience connects with the qualities they share with your main character. It can be physical, mental, emotional, or spiritual. It's a trait or aspect of the character that makes them different from everybody else in the story.

In the beginning of the story, it might not even seem very important, and maybe that's what the story is about: The main character doesn't fully appreciate or understand why they're unique and special.

Maybe it's an inner strength or will, or a secret that only the main character knows. Or the main character has a goodness, or a belief, that's different from everybody else. Or the main character is stronger, faster, smarter, funnier, or more outrageous in some way.

It doesn't matter. Just decide what your main character has that makes them different and special.

The reason for this is an important one.

It's because inside the hearts of the audience, they all want to be different and special, too. That's why your main character's struggles and achievements become so compelling to the audience. The audience wants to win the day in their own lives, too.

The Heroic Struggle

Finally, great main characters are also heroes. Audiences love stories that show a character fighting against overwhelming forces and becoming a hero.

These forces are the physical conflicts in the story the character does battle with. But the fight should also be personal and emotional. In the best movies, the main character is fighting inner problems as fiercely as the problems he or she is battling in the outside world.

In *The Matrix*, Neo is fighting himself as much as everything else. When he's rescued from his womb-like enslavement by Morpheus, Neo is presented with the shock of all shocks. What he thinks is reality is just a figment of his machine-controlled imagination.

For the rest of the movie, he struggles with his inability to believe in the truth, both about his world and himself. This inner struggle stops him from becoming "the one." That is, the one person who can be the hero of all heroes and save the human race.

At some point in your story, your main character should make a decision that puts him or her on the road to becoming a hero. It's a decision to do whatever it takes to win. The odds against her will of course be staggering. That's why main characters have to use everything in their power to vanquish what stands in their way. The intensity of the fight and the enormity of the personal challenges your character will have to overcome are what defines his or her heroic struggle.

Always remember, the audience loves heroes.

BLOCKBUSTER CHARACTERS CAN COME IN ANY PACKAGE

As said before, your main character can come in a variety of shapes and sizes. What will make him great is your ability to put him in a special and compelling light.

The audience has to believe in and care about your main character.

Following are three very different kinds of characters who might not normally be thought of as blockbuster heroes. None of them are wise-cracking, fist-throwing tough guys. But each, in a unique way, connected with a huge movie audience—and that's the real definition of a great main character.

Macaulay Culkin in *Home Alone*

This was a surprising blockbuster movie that exceeded all expectations.

The reason is the very simple but entertaining concept. Kevin is an eight-year-old boy who feels totally neglected and goofed-on by his big, hectic family. Then he's accidentally left at home when they all rush off for a Christmas vacation in Paris.

Kevin's dramatic "wants" in the story are very clear. He wants the respect and love of his family, but as the runt, he always gets the short end of the stick. And when a couple of burglars show up, he wants to foil their robbery attempts.

Kevin ends up protecting the house against the low-life burglars in a slapstick, cartoon-like showdown that's a kid-dream come true. Kevin becomes a hero using his special kid ingenuity. At the end of the movie, when he reunites with his family, he also receives the love and admiration he's always wanted.

Shrek in *Shrek*

In the animated movie *Shrek*, the audience was presented with a kind of main character they hadn't encountered before.

Shrek was a giant, grumpy ogre who preferred being alone because he hated everybody else. And you couldn't blame him. After all, ogres don't get any smiles or friendly slaps on the back when they stomp through their day. Shrek knew that everybody hated him, so he decided the feeling was more than mutual.

Except this wasn't the real Shrek.

In the story, he's sent off to rescue a beautiful princess locked away in a far-off castle. When he scoops up the princess and they begin their adventurous journey back, the real Shrek begins to emerge.

It turns out, underneath all that blubbery, puke-green skin, he's got an honest-to-goodness heart. He was just shielding his inner pain with a bad-guy attitude.

Shrek falls in love with princess.

After many surprises and great danger, all ends happily. Shrek becomes a hero and the audience loves him for it. He's an outsider who finds true love and acceptance against overwhelming odds.

Which is exactly what he's always secretly wanted.

Tom Hanks in *Forrest Gump*

Probably no blockbuster movie in recent history has as memorable a main character as Forest Gump. In fact, the success of the movie is due to the strong appeal of the title character. He touched the audience in a very deep and poignant way, all because of his strengths and weaknesses.

Forest was born with a low I.Q. This was his weakness. He simply wasn't as smart everybody else. He was slow. But he didn't let that define his life, because he had other special talents, too.

Forest Gump ended up using his inner spirit to make his life remarkable. He could have ended up a sad and lonely outcast, but he didn't. He faced all the hardships and bad luck that life threw at him with good humor and courage.

The story was a wonderfully heartfelt tale about a character who heroically rises above his limited abilities to live a life filled with love and hope.

It was the best kind of story in which a special hero overcomes all the countless challenges that come his way.

Creating a Main Character

Your main character is truly the heart and soul of your screenplay. In the following, the screenwriters talk about how they construct an effective main character. They agree that even though your main character is a hero, the quality the audience usually responds to is a weakness that makes them more human and appealing.

PHILIP EISNER *(Event Horizon)*

Audiences like heroes that have vulnerability. I think that's one of the things that really helped Arnold Schwarzenegger's career. Between *The Terminator* and *Terminator 2*, he did *Predator*. In that movie they turned around and asked, "What can kick Arnold's ass?" The alien is bigger than Arnold. Arnold can't out punch or out fight it. It made him more likable and vulnerable.

In *Die Hard* there's a great vulnerability to Bruce Willis, too. During most of the movie he's barefoot and it really increases his vulnerability. At the end of the movie, it's a great moment when he comes out to meet his wife. He's been shot, he's bloody, and every inch of his body has been beaten and battered. And the fact that what's driving him is very basic, the love of his wife, is something the audience connects with.

DAVID GOYER *(Blade)*

On a certain level, the audience has to identify with your main character. There's also an element of wish fulfillment. I know when I was growing up I used to fantasize about being the character in the movies I loved.

I think when you're dealing with your protagonist, they have to be flawed, because it makes them more relatable. Your hero should have a flaw and something they have to overcome, both personally and in terms of the greater world.

DAVID HAYTER *(X-Men)*

The key to creating a great main character, for me, is the balance between real and interesting. Especially in an action movie, you want your heroes to react, in the same way your audience would react so they're believable. They need to have an emotional life and a decision-making process that completely conforms to our own. That way, the audience can also put themselves into the story and go through the adventure, too.

At the same time, you want your main character to be interesting beyond the sort of dull reality we meet every day. You want to create a character that's a bit wild and extreme. You want them to have certain idiosyncrasies that are larger than life, more interesting than real life.

But you also don't want to go too far so the character becomes a cartoon.

JIM KOUF *(Rush Hour)*

One of the tricks I've learned is that the audience will always like a character with a sense of humor. I always try to have my main character have one. It shows another side of the character. It always helps the movie, too.

BLOCKBUSTER STORIES GO PLACES

*"I've seen things you people
wouldn't believe."*
—Bladerunner

Blockbuster stories strive to be new and unique, so they're all different.

As we've discussed though, they also share common elements that make them accessible and entertaining to the widest possible audience. They're stories that engage the heart, the mind, and the imagination. They also have a main character the audience can relate to in a way that's personal and specific.

There's also another broader technique that can be enormously helpful in creating a story audiences will feel a deep connection to.

THE JOURNEY STORY STRUCTURE

The journey story structure is a wonderful creative tool for the blockbuster screenwriter. It's a simple way to optimize your big idea's appeal to the audience. It will give your story scope, structure, and pace, and will also helps to pull the audience "into the world of your story." The audience is taken on a journey that has a beginning, a middle, and an end.

But it's the events that happen on this journey that can make it a great blockbuster movie.

Joseph Campbell, in his book *The Hero with a Thousand Faces*, goes into depth about the importance of the "journey structure" to stories. From his study of myths and legends, and their psychological connections to the audience, he explains how all stories have a similar structure, and it's one of the key reasons for their enduring appeal.

An understanding of Campbell's story structure and narrative model is helpful to any dramatic writer. Both George Lucas and Steven Spielberg have acknowledged Campbell's work as a specific and influential inspiration for their movies.

There are two broad characteristics of the journey story structure that are especially important for blockbuster movies: spectacle and spirit.

THE JOURNEY HAS SPECTACLE

In real life, a journey takes you away from your normal life to a place that's new, exotic, mysterious, and strange. Spectacle is anything that hits you with new experiences and visuals that challenge your usual assumptions and habits. On a journey with spectacle,the sights and sounds are different. The terrain is different. Everything is different. So it forces you to think, act, and be different.

Spectacle is a quality you want in your screenplay, because it takes the audience to a place they've never been and shows them sights they've never seen.

Remember, the movie screen is big, so you want to create a story that takes characters to a place where there's something special to look at.

But it doesn't have to be on a distant planet a gazillion miles away (*Planet of the Apes*); spectacle can also be found in an ordinary suburban bedroom (*Poltergeist* and *Toy Story*), or in a backyard (*Honey, I Shrunk the Kids*), or even inside one of the characters (*Innerspace*).

Spectacle can be anything that's fun, exhilarating, horrific, outrageous, or startling.

In the journey story structure, your characters venture off to a place that's also dangerous in some way.

It's filled with enemies, traps, attacks, hidden dangers and battles. These are the conflicts in your story.

But the journey doesn't have to be a physical one. It can also be metaphorical. It can be a journey that takes place in the heart, the mind, or the soul. The characters don't even have to leave their house, as in the examples just cited, but something in their world must change to create challenges and tests for them to face.

Blockbuster movies have characters physically or psychologically braving a sudden change in their lives that's radically different from anything they've ever experienced before. When developing your movie story, push yourself to tell it with visual images and sequences that include spectacle.

In an action movie that means inventing new action set-pieces and sequences that are breathless and imaginative. If you're writing a horror movie, look for new ways to startle and frighten an audience with scares that are yanked even deeper from the subconscious. If you're writing a romantic comedy, it means inventing fresh and funny ways to dramatize the awkward dance of falling in love.

The goal is to create bold and visually exciting new ways to tell your story.

THE JOURNEY IS SPIRITUAL

The best blockbuster movies are also a journey of the spirit.

They have soul.

The spiritual journey awakens or reconfigures a character's innermost spirit and sense-of-self. The inner world of the character is changed in some way when you take them beyond the comfort-zone of their everyday lives and they're challenged to their most extreme limits. Blockbuster movies are never about what's modest, meek, or mild. They're about characters facing their most dreaded fears and being challenged to their utmost breaking-point. It's this tenacity and courage to overcome all obstacles that connects a character with the audience on the deepest level.

This spiritual awakening can be the emergence of a character's heroic persona, a deeper understanding of what's been missing from the character's life, or some other kind of soul-changing insight or revelation.

The journey story structure is also an effective way to dramatize characters struggling with their innermost demons and desires, because audiences connect with this, too. The audience wants the characters in your story to be spiritually renewed and transformed, because that's what they seek in their own lives. The giant glowing, scenes on the screen, if written effectively, will cause the audience to feel an inner glow, too.

That's what makes a movie a blockbuster.

City Slickers

MOVIE CLOSE-UP

In the movie *City Slickers*, the screenwriters Lowell Ganz and Babaloo Mandel used the journey story structure wonderfully.

Billy Crystal plays the main character, Mitch Robbins. With his fortieth birthday quickly approaching, Mitch realizes his life has fallen into a major middle-aged rut. In spiritual terms, he's running out of gas, so he takes off with his two best friends for a pick-me-up getaway at a dude ranch to get his inner motor running again.

It's a vacation-journey from civilized city living to the wide open spaces of the Midwest, where their normal skills don't apply anymore. During a long-distance cattle drive, the three border-line wimpy city guys are truly tested for the first time in their lives. They face all kinds of rough-and-tumble dangers and hardships.

They're also in a landscape that opens their blurry city eyes to spectacular new sights and fresh-air vistas. They've journeyed to a place where men are men, and wimps aren't welcome. Along the way, the three best friends rediscover a part of their inner spirit they'd all lost touch with.

At the end of the trip, Mitch has visibly changed, and his soul has been renewed. By enduring the extreme challenges of the journey away from his city comfort-zone, he gets his confidence and zest for life back.

The movie is a very funny and exciting adventure story that's part rollicking western, part neurotic urban comedy. But most of all, it's a spiritual and spectacular journey for the characters that the audience loved.

PART THREE

WRITING A MILLION DOLLAR SCREENPLAY

START WITH A
BIG IDEA AND BUILD

"If you build it, they will come."
Field of Dreams

Writing a blockbuster screenplay isn't as hard as you think.

What's hard is creating the story.

All successful screenwriters know the hands-down toughest part of screenwriting is taking the original idea and developing it into a great story. Once you've done that, then writing the screenplay is usually not as difficult a creative process.

Up until now, we've talked about why you need a big idea as a new and bold launch pad for your screenplay. But just having a big idea is not what makes you a blockbuster screenwriter. It's only the beginning.

CREATING A STORY

Turning that idea into a story is a much different process. It's a more formal undertaking that draws on your creative talent but also requires a solid understanding of dramatic structure. You can get a big idea in a flash of inspiration, but turning that idea into story is always a more rigorous and time-consuming exercise. For the screenwriter, this is where the creative heavy lifting is done.

A great movie idea is always a beautiful and exciting concept to consider. It sparkles and glows with entertainment possibilities.

For you, the screenwriter, your talent and dramatic skill is what's going to turn that idea into a blockbuster story that sizzles with excitement.

The story you create is what it's all about. Even the most megaton-big idea will fizzle and sputter if it's put in a poorly constructed story. In the movie world it's called "execution." Execution is the ability to take an idea and turn it into a story that has plot, pace, and all the other dramatically powerful elements that audiences love: *Surprises. Action. Danger. Comedy. Thrills. Twists and turns. Emotionally driven characters facing life-changing challenges*. While the idea is crucial, the story you create from the idea is what the audience will actually see on that screen.

Great blockbuster ideas can come from anywhere, as the following story illustrates. As a writer, you have to always be open to inspiration. But the challenge remains the same, and that's to take the original idea and craft it into a movie story that's filled with big screen excitement and entertainment.

FROM IDEA TO MILLION DOLLAR $ALE

Scott Rosenberg

My highest-selling million dollar spec sale was for a script called *The Ten*. I got the idea when I was home for Passover Seder one year. They always tell the story of the ten plagues. I remember sitting there while the story was being told and suddenly thinking, there's a movie in this.

It was just after all those disaster movies came out. There was *Volcano*, *Twister* and some others. I just knew this was a great idea. I remember being insanely afraid that I was going to pick up the trades and see that somebody else was already doing it.

I started thinking about a story. The idea I came up with was that a terrorist leader figures out a way to harness the ten plagues of Egypt. He holds all of America hostage. Each plague is going to strike a different American city unless the government releases the members of his organization.

I was in pre-production on *Con Air* at the time. I was working non-stop on that, so I didn't have time to write it. Then Jerry Bruckheimer came to me one day and said they wanted to bring in another writer to tackle some story problems we were having. He gave me a month off. That's when I wrote it.

I immediately gave it to my agent and she thought it was great. I remember being on the set of *Con Air* when it all went down. There's nothing more exciting. The Weinsteins at Miramax/Dimension were involved, along with Renny Harlin and New Line, and Mace Neufield and Paramount.

The offers started coming in. The final deal was complicated. It involved another earlier screenplay I'd written called *Bad Moon Rising*, about a werewolf motorcycle gang. The final figure was around $1.6 million.

The act of creation is always a mysterious and messy process. It doesn't matter if you're creating the universe, writing a poem, or making a hot dog.

Creating a blockbuster story is no different. It's mysterious because no two screenwriters think alike or have the same creative process. Every screenwriter has their own personal method for turning an idea into a story. It's messy because the imaginative quest for a new story is always one of trial-and-error. It's a mental wrestling match where ideas are thrown around with wild abandon. Some live, but lots usually die. It's not a pretty sight.

But the process always begins with a basic first step, which involves not making the mistake of writing your screenplay too quickly, before you're ready.

STORY PREPARATION

Preparation is the stage in the creative process when you let your movie idea grow on it's own without imposing any demands on it yet. Be loose, go with the creative flow wherever it takes you. You're still looking for ideas and inspiration that can kick your movie concept up to the next level: *a story*.

Turn On Your Story Radar

The first part of the process is the easiest. You put your movie idea in your head and leave it there.

That's all you do. You just let it float around in your brain. Because when you do this, you'll notice something immediately starts to happen.

Your idea begins to grow.

It's your mind and imagination at work. Often times, it happens without you even knowing it. Somewhere, in the mysterious inner-workings of your mind, as your imagination plays the role of mad scientist, your movie idea starts to come alive.

As you go through your daily routine, you'll also get other ideas from the world around you. An overheard conversation will spark an idea for a character. You'll read an article in a magazine that will suggest a great plot twist. The world itself will feed you a creative smorgasbord of ideas and inspiration, because your "story radar" has been switched on.

Some screenwriters carry their idea around for weeks, months, even years. During this time, the initial idea grows and grows, until it evolves into a story.

It may not be completely finished, with all the details worked out, but it will have a rough shape and tone.

For each project, most screenwriters have a notebook or some system to organize the rather messy and chaotic collection of ideas they gather during this stage of story development. Again, all writers work differently, but most have categories into which they divide the ideas: character, plot, background information, etc.

Research Helps

During this time, you also want to do any research that will inspire you further and give you factual material you can use in your story.

In your screenplay, you want to create a new world that's vivid and believable. Research helps you accomplish this. Read about the places and the kind of characters you'll be using in your story. Visit locations if it's possible. Clip out articles and pictures. Learn about anything that can stimulate your creativity with new notions and ideas.

As you do research, your story will grow even more and become more clear and real.

You don't want to fake your way through a story. If someone is reading your screenplay and the details are wrong, then the whole story is weakened. Research provides you with these details. Your screenplay has to be totally realistic in presenting the imaginary story you want to tell.

Anything That Inspires You Is Good

Don't be judgmental or demanding just yet. Go with your instincts and curiosities wherever they lead you.

The first stage is often the most fun. You've come up with a blockbuster movie idea that's filled with big-screen possibilities. Your excitement and imagination gets pumped up as ideas, characters, and visuals begin to come alive in your head.

What's best during this stage is not to impose any arbitrary structure on the process. Let your imagination run free for awhile. At the same time, seek out as much related information as you can. Read, see movies, visit art galleries, put Speedos on your curiosity and surf the Internet. Mostly, you just want to think and daydream about story possibilities.

Every movie idea has many different creative roads you can take. During this stage, you want to mentally wander these roads in the unstructured freedom of your imagination.

Some writers will sit in a chair and listen to music. Others will take a long walk, jog, swim, or sit in a park. It's doesn't matter, because the objective is the same.

Whatever works is fine. The key is to find an environment or activity that stimulates your creativity.

During this stage, you want your imagination and your movie idea to spend quality time together.

BLOCKBUSTER SCREENPLAYS ARE BUILT TO THRILL

"Awesome! Totally awesome!"
—Fast Times At Ridgemont High

After you've finished the preparation stage, it's time to take what you've come up with and shape it more clearly into a story.

You do this with "story structure." Story structure is the organizational blueprint for your screenplay. It's the basic model for how to tell a story that comes from the history of storytelling.

It's what works.

Blockbuster movies, like movies in general, use "three-act-dramatic structure." The purpose of structure is to make sure the dramatic elements and events in a story are organized in the best way possible. It's a relatively simple set of guidelines and principles that helps shape your initial concept into a story.

More specifically, structure is what's going to transform the haphazard collection of notes and ideas you've gathered into a blockbuster screenplay that delivers the goods.

THREE-ACT DRAMATIC STRUCTURE

A screenplay is generally between 100 and 120 pages. The accepted rule of thumb is one page equals one minute of screen time. In broad terms, three-act structure is this:

ACT ONE (pages 1–30) is the introduction. In this section the important dramatic elements in the story are introduced and established: tone, setting, characters, and conflict.

At the end of Act One, the reader has to know who the story is about, what the story is about, when it takes place, and where.

ACT TWO (pages 30–90) is the confrontation between your main character, or characters, and the conflict. The struggle escalates in intensity. At the end of Act Two, the reader is emotionally invested in the story and desperately wants to know who's going to win.

ACT THREE (pages 90–110) is the climax. The confrontation between the main character and the conflict is resolved. There's a winner and a loser.

This is the basic structure you should use. For a blockbuster story, though, you also want all the individual elements to be as big and bold as possible. You're going for maximum entertainment. There's nothing meek or modest about a blockbuster movie.

Sure, there are going to be quiet moments and story subtlety. You don't want to write a screenplay that's just a mindless parade of explosions and car chases. That would be simplistic and not very entertaining. It also wouldn't be a blockbuster story, because it's not a story.

Don't mistake non-stop action and special effects for exciting storytelling. Remember, the heart of a great story is emotionally compelling characters who experience challenges the audience can connect with.

Being big and bold is about maximizing every dramatic element to its fullest potential. It's about being imaginatively majestic in your storytelling.

Some screenwriting gurus and how-to books like to over-theorize about exactly what has to happen at each stage of the story. They present a very clearly marked map about what the story should be, every step along the way.

If you want to be a blockbuster screenwriter, that's the wrong road to take.

Don't obsessively follow any formulas or overly detailed rules for telling your story. Structure is a set of guidelines that are meant to be helpful, not iron-clad and suffocating.

Blockbuster screenwriters are explorers and risk-takers. They search for new narrative roads and exhilarating ways to tell a story the audience has never seen before.

The following section is a detailed breakdown of the revved-up story structure that blockbuster stories strive for. While not all of these elements will apply to every screenplay, understanding this overall structure can be helpful in turning your big idea into a million dollar story.

BLOCKBUSTER THREE-ACT STRUCTURE

ACT ONE

In Act One you introduce and dramatically establish the key

elements in your story. In blockbuster storytelling you want to do this as entertainingly as possible. Nothing should be hum-drum or the way it's usually done. Act One should be a one-of-a-kind lift-off for your blockbuster screenplay.

Start with a Story Hook

Like everything else in a blockbuster movie, your first ten pages have to be awesome.

First, they need to establish the tone of your story. If you're writing an action-adventure story, those first ten pages should show what you can do: write an action sequence that's spectacular and electrifying.

Think about the beginning of a James Bond or an Indiana Jones movie. All have great opening sequences that use exotic locations and big-screen action to establish the scope and tone of the story. The opening sequences are always mini-thrill-rides, with the hero immediately facing a horrible and certain death. James and Indiana always manage to escape, of course, with the promise of even bigger thrills to come.

In the same way, if you're writing a wild comedy, there better be something outrageous and funny right away that tells the audience what kind of movie they're going to see. The same for a horror movie, a thriller, an historical epic, a love story, or anything else.

Most of all, no matter what kind of movie you're writing, you have to hook the audience's heart and eyeballs from the very beginning. There needs to be something in the beginning of your screenplay that announces: HANG ON, THIS IS GOING TO BE A HELL OF A RIDE!

Remember that your audience includes the people who will first read your screenplay. That's another reason the opening of your story is so important. Many agents and other industry people won't read past the first ten or twenty pages if they're not hooked into the story. For a blockbuster movie, you want to start big and keep getting bigger.

Whether they feature action, emotions, mysteries, scares,

or comedy, blockbuster movies start with a bang and keep exploding after that.

Independence Day

Dean Devlin and Roland Emmerich created a simple but powerful opening scene for *Independence Day*. The movie is a good guys vs. bad guys story, with humans and aliens fighting for planet Earth like cosmic gunfighters. The movie opens on the surface of the moon. We see a tiny plaque that reads,  "One small step for a man, one giant leap for mankind." The plaque, of course, symbolizes a pretty nifty achievement for mankind.

Then a humongous black shadow suddenly rumbles overhead. It's headed towards Earth. The message is clear: HEY, EARTH, SOMETHING BIG AND BAD IS COMING YOUR WAY...

Introduce Us to a Strange New World

As stated before, audiences love to be taken to places that are strange, exotic, and new. Whenever we leave our normal surroundings, there's always an underlying mood of anticipation and excitement. The usual rules and expectations don't apply anymore. There's a feeling anything can happen.

During the first act of your screenplay, you want to establish a visual setting that communicates this feeling to the audience. You want the audience to feel they've left their comfort-zone behind. The normal rules don't apply. In the immortal words of a young farm girl, the audience should know they're not in Kansas anymore. Your story landscape should suggest these possibilities as soon as possible.

The new world you introduce in your story can be anywhere: a bustling big city, a sleepy suburban town, a top-secret outpost in outer space. But no matter where your story takes place, the setting should evoke a feeling that strange and unexpected events can occur.

It needs to be different, mysterious, offbeat, or bizarre—though not necessarily on the outside, where everything can appear normal. It can be underneath the surface in some way.

Take a sleepy small-town. We see the usual sights. Lots of normal-looking houses with white picket fences. Kids are riding bicycles. A pleasant looking man is watering his lawn. Some of you probably grew up in a town like this. It looks like a nice place to live, but not a place where anything very exciting or thrilling would ever happen.

Unless, course, it's the town in the movie *Jumanji*, when a children's board game unleashes a thundering stampede of ferocious wild animals that turns the sleepy town into a chaotic, heart-pounding jungle of life-threatening dangers.

Or it could be the perfect-looking town in *The Truman Show*, which turns out to be anything but perfect, because it's not even a real town—it's the giant set for a TV show.

In both of these places, the audience quickly realized anything could happen.

First Impressions Count

The hero of your movie deserves a great introduction. Your main character is the force that drives your story and carries the audience along. Blockbuster screenwriters always introduce their main character with a clear dramatic message: *Pay attention to this person.*

You do that with some kind of dramatic sizzle or spotlight. Make the first time we meet the hero of your story interesting, unexpected, unique, flashy, or emotionally powerful. Put them at the center of a dramatic event that sets them apart from everybody else. They have to be different or special in some way. If they're not, then they shouldn't be the focus of a blockbuster story.

What's special about your main character? Is it what's on the outside that sets them apart? Maybe they have a mission, talent, or responsibility that's integral to the story. Or is it something on the inside? An emotional want or desire can also drive the action.

Whatever it is, this is what you should think about when you're creating a movie entrance for your hero. Decide what aspect of their character defines their dramatic value to the story and then showcase it in a great scene or sequence. Think of it as creating a dramatic red carpet that announces what's special about your hero.

Remember, the most important element for an audience is usually your hero. Audiences vicariously experience the movie through your hero's eyes. We're all the center of our own world, and that's the way your hero should be presented in the story. The story is important because of what it means to your main character.

A good introduction reveals right away the essence of your hero. It illustrates what drives her to be who she is, or what keeps him from being the best he can be.

A polite introduction is rarely effective. Be edgy, surprising, outrageous, emotional, mysterious, funny, or shocking. The heart and soul of your hero is also going to be the heart and soul of your blockbuster story.

Batman

In *Batman*, the screenwriter Sam Hamm created an introduction that established his hero's dark and vengeful persona.

Batman first appears high above a city beneath a moonlight night sky. He descends out of the darkness like a human gargoyle to help a family that's been terrorized and robbed. He confronts the scummy thugs in a way that quickly shows his superhero stuff, but it also becomes apparent that Batman is a little creepy himself, witha menacing voice and a sinister attitude.

This is a perfect introduction, because these are the qualities that give the movie it's moody, spooky tone. Batman is a heroic crime fighter, but he's also emotionally haunted. He's dedicated his life to doing good, but he doesn't feel all that good himself.

The Last Boy Scout

In *The Last Boy Scout*, the screenwriter Shane Black introduced his hero in a much different way.

In the movie, Bruce Willis plays Joe Hallenbeck, a small-time private investigator. When we first meet him, though, he's anything but heroic. He's a broken-down drunk who wakes up in his car with a dead squirrel on his chest. He's literally hit rock bottom in every way imaginable. Everybody hates him, including himself. He's all the way down and almost out.

In this case, what's important about the character is his shattered inner self, before he fights back. The screenwriter created an introduction that showed a good man in a very dark place. The movie is about his epic climb back to being a hero.

Something Wicked this Way Comes

In the first act, you also introduce your villain, or main conflict, with the same kind of dramatic energy and effectiveness. Again, be imaginative and bold.

Whatever it is—a vicious villain, a runaway meteor, a planet threatening biological plague—create an introduction that rattles the world of your story and rattles the audience, too.

You want the audience to have an emotional reaction to the first appearance of your villain or conflict. The scene should connect with their fears and give big-screen warning that a blockbuster "bad guy" has arrived.

In many screenplays, in fact, it's the conflict or villain that gives the story its blockbuster identity. The conflict is some predatory new force that suddenly rises up in an unsuspecting landscape. So the first time it appears, the tone and mood of the story should be shaken up, too.

Think about what makes your conflict dangerous. What's the essence of its ability to do harm and instill fear? Usually this is primal in nature. It has the power to wreck havoc and destruction in some physical or emotional way.

Again, it doesn't matter what kind of story you're writing. It can be a gross-out comedy with teenagers, or a historical fantasy with knights and magicians. Locate the source of your conflict's power, then create a story introduction that dramatizes this in the most vivid and interesting way possible. It should be the first rumble of an earthquake that's going to rock-and-roll your hero's world.

In *Twister*, the conflict is tornadoes. In the opening scene, a family rushes to the cellar of their house as a tornado comes blasting through. For a moment or two, they appear to be safe, but then the father is suddenly yanked away, sucked up into the sky like a flimsy little doll, by the unbelievable power of the colossal storm.

You can also hook the audience with apprehension and mystery. *Jaws* introduced its blockbuster bad guy by keeping its identity a secret at first. A young girl paddles out for a late night swim and is suddenly, savagely devoured by something below. This is effective because Carl Gottlieb, the screenwriter, played on people's fundamental fear of sharks. They can be secretly lurking in the watery depths below at any time of day or night.

With some stories though, you might want to introduce your conflict or villain in "sheep's clothing" at first. In *Fatal Attraction* the villain is initially seen as a beautiful and sexy woman out for some sneaky adult fun. But then she suddenly turns psycho when her married male partner decides it's time to move on. This opening works because it's part of the primal fear of becoming involved with a stranger. The fear is that the stranger may be a hell of a lot stranger than you bargained for.

The Battle Begins

At the end of Act One, the stage has been set and the audience is ready for the blockbuster battle to begin. They're inching toward the edges of their seats. Their hearts are pounding a little faster. They've met a hero they can cheer for and a villain they can boo.

They know they've entered a story-world where exciting and surprising things can happen.

Now it's time to blow them away.

ACT TWO

The battle between your hero and the conflict is the main event of your blockbuster story.

This is what happens in Act Two.

Here, movie heroes must travel, either physically or metaphorically, away from home into a dangerous and threatening new landscape. Along the way, they meet friends and helpers while confronting unexpected challenges and conflicts that grow in magnitude and intensity.

Act Two is the biggest section of your screenplay, so it's usually the most difficult to develop and write. You have to use your talent and imagination to the fullest. The second act of your screenplay has to swing for the fence in every way possible. It has to be a maxed-out tour-de-force of big-screen entertainment. The audience must be taken on a heart-thumping ride that has more twists and thrills than a Disney World rollercoaster.

That's the goal. That's what you shoot for.

Think of *The Matrix*, *The Mummy*, or *XXX*. They all had second acts that kept pushing the thrill-meter and spectacle level higher and higher. You don't want anybody in the audience yawning or stumbling off to the concession stand or bathroom during Act Two. If they do, then your talent and imagination haven't done their jobs. The audience should be super-glued to their seats, breathless to see what surprise your hero will face next. They should be so involved in the story that everything else fades away.

In Act Two, here are the blockbuster story elements to consider:

The Conflict Gets Stronger

The conflict or villain is truly the life blood of your story in the second act. It's what keeps the narrative pumped up and flowing. Without a powerful and crafty conflict that grows and confounds the hero's efforts, your story will not rise to it's highest level of intensity and entertainment. If the conflict does not get stronger and more antagonistic as Act Two plays out, then the hero will not be challenged to their utmost. This is the dramatic essence of a blockbuster movie: Your hero must be challenged to the outermost limits of his abilities and endurance.

Think about your Act Two as a visual, high-concept chess game between your main character and the conflict. It's not as low-key, of course, but the goal is the same. Each side uses whatever their individual strength and power is to win.

The battle should never be depicted as even and fair though. At some point, the conflict should be seen as an adversarial "Goliath" that keeps getting bigger and more powerful. Your hero is a struggling "David" that seems almost certainly the loser. As Act Two develops, this David and Goliath battle draws the audience in with every mismatched face-off and entanglement.

In *The Perfect Storm*, this is illustrated with staggering visual power. The heroes are a small group of fishermen taking their boat out to sea. In the second act, they suddenly find themselves caught in the path of "a perfect storm." As the second act progresses, the size and monster-like rage of the storm grows and so does the intensity of the audience's emotions for the crew.

In the *The Terminator*, the villain is a cyborg from the future with a mission to kill. In this case, the relentless indestructibility of the human-looking cyborg drives the story forward. No matter what the heroes try, the cyborg continues to pursue them like a murderous, unstoppable juggernaut.

In both cases, the main characters face conflicts that are visually vivid and profoundly antagonistic. The heroes do their best, but the villain is always much stronger. The heroes must dig deeper and deeper into their inner resources to find a way to win. During Act Two, the conflict evolves and grows, forcing the heroes to do the same.

THE HERO IS FIGHTING FOR HIS LIFE Blockbuster stories are usually for the biggest stakes possible, and there's nothing bigger than fighting for your life. The prospect of death is a fear that unites us all, so it's always a compelling story for an audience to watch. It's also why so many blockbuster movies involve intense physical jeopardy for the characters. It's simply the most dramatic predicament possible for a character in a movie.

In fact, this kind of storytelling can be traced back to an earlier prototype for blockbuster movies, the Saturday morning serial. These stories are all constructed around a plot device called "the cliff-hanger." At the end of each episode, the hero is invariably trapped in a situation in which death appears certain and imminent, like hanging from the edge of a cliff or being tied to railroad tracks in front of an oncoming train. Needless to say, audiences returned the following Saturday to see if the brawny hero or dainty damsel lived or died. George Lucas and Steven Spielberg both cite Saturday morning serials and their cliff-hanger narrative style as the inspiration for the *Indiana Jones* movies.

If you're writing the kind of blockbuster story that involves action and danger, then pull out all the stops in Act Two. Your hero should be put in the line of fire time and time again. Put a dramatic bulls-eye on their butt and blast away.

Try to be new and imaginative with the kinds of life-threatening scenes and sequences you create. The audience doesn't need to yawn through another generic car chase or fistfight. Make your showdowns and entanglements bigger and bolder.

There's nothing more gripping to an audience than watching a hero they've identified with fighting for his or her life. If this kind of scenario is part of your story, then showcase it as intensely as you can in Act Two.

Of course, not all blockbuster stories are about a life-and-death battles. Some present a fight about other things. But here's what's always important: During Act Two, your main character or hero should be fighting for something *he can't afford to lose.*

If it's not for his life, then it needs to be almost as important. Your main character has to battle for something that's fundamental to her world and deeply important. Because only then will the stakes be high enough for your story to have emotional power and depth. Blockbuster movies are about big battles and big stakes.

Ghost

MOVIE CLOSE-UP Bruce Joel Rubin, the screenwriter of *Ghost*, wrote a very successful movie about a hero the audience knew right away wasn't fighting for his life. That's because he was already dead. Patrick Swayze, the hero of the story, was savagely murdered at the beginning of the movie.

So what did he fight for if he was already dead?

He fought for the woman he loved.

The movie is about a character facing what appears to be an insurmountable obstacle. The conflict was death itself. If you're dead, how do you still protect the people you love? In this case, it was the hero's love that gave the movie its emotional power. The audience felt his heartbreaking pain at not being able to "break through to the other side." He wasn't fighting for his own life, but he was fighting for something equally important. He was fighting for the woman who gave his life meaning. If he failed, it was obvious the pain would be impossible to bear. Even in death.

This example suggests another quality you should consider for your main character.

THE HERO IS FIGHTING FOR SOMEBODY ELSE, TOO

During Act Two, as your hero fights the conflict or villain, it's always better if he's not doing so purely out of self-interest. If your main character is only motivated by personal welfare and needs, it diminishes his or her appeal to the audience.

The reason is simple. Heroes fight for other people, not just themselves. That's what a hero does. It doesn't matter if it's a stranger, a family, or the entire population of the planet. Your main character should be emotionally connected to somebody else in the story and be fighting for that character as well.

THE ACTION GROWS IN INTENSITY

As Act Two develops, your hero is fighting through a blockbuster obstacle-course that's filled with missteps, frustrations, and failure. There will be small victories, sure, but during Act Two, your main character should experience the pain of losing, because that's what will make them stronger.

During Act Two, the villain or conflict forces your hero to dig deeper inside himself to discover his true power. It may be courage, strength of will, or knowledge, but it's been missing from his life and now he needs it to survive. Your main character has to overcome whatever inner roadblocks or illusions he's had and become what he was always meant to be.

As Act Two plays out, the obstacles and challenges for your main character get bigger and more ferocious. The pace of the story quickens. The intensity grows. The audience is pumped up with anticipation. And all of this hinges on the answer to a single question: Is the story going to have a happy ending or a sad one?

SURPRISES, REVELATIONS, NEW IDEAS

Along the way, the best blockbuster movies have great surprises and plot turns. In Act Two, the world of the story keeps growing and evolving with excitement, challenges, mysteries, and complexity.

In a blockbuster movie, boring is always bad, because it leads to predictability, which is an instant audience turn-off. In order to avoid this, you do the same thing with the audience as you do with your main character. *Take them out of their comfort-zone.* The audience can never feel they know what direction the story is headed or feel superior to the storytelling in any way. Like any great thrill-ride, you want the audience to have their mental seatbelts on tight, because they don't know what's going to happen from one second to the next.

SURPRISES (ALSO CALLED TWISTS AND TURNS) jolt the audience with the unexpected. Every surprise jars the audience away from their assumptions about the story.

When an audience begins to anticipate where the story is going, they get complacent, they think they've got the story figured out. If that happens and the audience is right, then you haven't written a blockbuster movie.

Blockbuster movies are never about what's probable and expected. They're always about what's surprising and startling. Surprises keep the audience glued to the screen, because they don't know what's going to happen next.

In *Thelma & Louise*, Susan Sarandon and Geena Davis play two small-town friends on the run from the law who pick up a handsome young hitch-hiker, played by Brad Pitt. Everything is fine until he secretly sneaks away with all their money and leaves them flat-broke.

This plot surprise pushes the story in a direction that intensifies the pressure on the two desperado friends. Now, they have to live by their own rules if they want to survive.

REVELATIONS are story secrets and mysteries that are revealed and answered. A revelation dramatically exposes information that enriches the audience's understanding of what the story is really about. It connects the dots. Revelations are glimpses into a deeper truth about the world of the story that put everything into a clearer light. The blockbuster screenwriter uses revelations to highlight essential truths that aren't readily visible on the surface of the story.

One of the most famous examples of this occurs in *Star Wars* when it's revealed that Darth Vader is Luke's father. Some story revelations are so important and startling they're kept hidden until even later as a final dramatic jolt, as in *Fight Club*, when the audience learns the brain-twisting truth about the relationship between the two main characters. Story revelations can be one of the most powerful and exciting effects in a screenwriter's bag-of-tricks. At some point in Act Two, a deeper secret or mystery about the story should be revealed.

NEW IDEAS are important too. The best blockbuster movies bring in big new ideas in Act Two. It can be about the world of the story, the characters, or anything else. As a blockbuster storyteller, your Second Act should be an expanding series of discoveries to keep the audience engaged. Don't get lazy. Once you've introduced all the key elements in Act One, keep pushing yourself to make the world of the story exciting and evolving.

The *Star Wars* series also does this terrifically. In each movie, Act Two always blasts off to far flung new worlds that continually reinvigorate the imaginative and visual appeal of the story. The audience is treated to an action-packed romp through alien landscapes that keep the big screen teeming with new ideas and spectacle. For instance, in *Star Wars: The Phantom Menace*, the action takes the characters to a wildly different array of otherworldly locations, from the parched and dusty desert planet of Tatooine, to Otah Gunga, the shimmering underwater city of giant jewel-like globes.

Even if you're not writing a galactic adventure story, make sure new story ideas continue to appear in Act Two.

THEME Act Two is also when the theme of your story should appear. All stories are about something universal to the human condition, and blockbuster stories are no different. The theme is what the story means to the audience on a personal level. Theme is what the movie is saying about life and how it should be lived. Usually, in a blockbuster movie, the theme speaks to the fundamental question that's at the heart of the human experience:

In a world filled with colossal challenges, how can a single individual survive and succeed?

In *Spiderman*, the main character is a teenager who accidentally gets super-hero powers. For awhile, his life is a nerd's dream come true. He sprouts rippling muscles, he can swing from soaring buildings with the greatest of ease, hot girls start to dig him. But as the story evolves, he also discovers that even the life of a super-hero provokes soul-searching questions that have to be answered. What he begins to realize in Act Two is the theme of the movie: *With great power also comes great responsibility*.

ACT THREE

Act Three is a blockbuster ending that takes everything in the story that came before and builds to an audience-thrilling, fight-to-the-finish finale. The audience has watched the images you've created for that giant glowing screen, and they've come to care about the characters they've been watching in the dark. You've taken them on a journey that has surprises, revelations, pain and joy. It's a story that has pulled them into the strange and spectacular new world you imagined in your head.

So what do you do now?

Now You Really Blow Them Away

Your ending is when it all comes together and your story rises to its highest point of intensity and blockbuster excitement.

Up until now, your hero has been fighting up a steep and torturous story slope against overwhelming odds. As he nears the top, he's exhausted, drained, running on empty. Your hero should then discover the torturous slope he's been on leads to the top of a mountain. Except it's not a mountain. It's a volcano.

And it begins to erupt . . .

And all the story thrills that came before are less so compared to what's now blazing on the screen. Whether it's a comedy, drama, or any other genre, Act Three takes everything you've already done and makes it better. It lifts the story to a final, crowd-pleasing finish that that will already have the audience cheering for a sequel.

But all this will happen only if Acts One and Two have been dramatically effective. The audience has to be fully engaged in the world of the story. They have to believe in it totally and completely. They have to care about the characters you've created, especially your main character or hero. If you've done your job as a blockbuster screenwriter, the audience will now be rooting for the hero to win.

They'll want this desperately.

You want the audience to care deeply about how the story is going to end. An effective ending has an impact on both the characters' lives and the lives of the audience. If the audience has truly identified with the hero, they will feel what the hero feels at the end of the story. If the story has a tragic ending, then the audience will feel that tragedy in a genuine and emotional way. If it's a happy ending, then the audience will leave the movie theater with smiles. Being happy is more enjoyable, of course, which is why so many blockbuster movies have rousing, rip-roaring endings in which the hero emerges from a cloud of smoke as the final victor and winner.

Following are key story techniques that will help make your ending effective.

THE OUTCOME IS UNPREDICTABLE One of the strongest sensations an audience should feel in the story should come right before the climax. It's heart-pounding anticipation. They want to know if the hero is going to win or lose, and this question has to be one the audience honestly does not know the answer to. They may have a hunch, or certainly a hope, but they have to be anxiously waiting for the story itself to answer this question.

Like any other part of a blockbuster story, if the audience guesses too quickly what the climax of the movie is, and it turns out they're right, then the story hasn't fulfilled it's obligation of being an unpredictable ride from beginning to end. The best blockbuster movies often save their biggest surprise for last.

THERE'S A TICKING CLOCK One sure-fire way to push the climax to maximum intensity is to have a "ticking clock" element involved. This is when your main character or hero has to achieve a specific objective within a limited period of time or all is lost. Both *Independence Day* and *Armageddon* used this technique as part of their save-the-world story climaxes.

The ticking clock device is a very effective way to concentrate the dramatic stakes at the end of the story with a non-negotiable deadline. It focuses and makes more vivid the pressure on the hero. It's now or never. Do or die. It all comes down to this. Tick, tick, tick . . .

THE FINAL SHOWDOWN IS FACE-TO-FACE By the end of the movie, the audience has come to identify with the hero so completely that they've also developed an equally strong feeling about the villain or conflict. It's been building with every fight, battle, and setback the hero has had to endure.

At the end of the movie, the audience wants the hero to not only win, they want to slide out to the very edge of their seat, power down the rest of their popcorn, and watch the hero win big in a face-to-face fight. It's a purely emotional feeling. They want the good-guy to win, and they want to see him do it in a one-on-one confrontation in which all the inner anger they've built up while watching the movie is vicariously released.

The audience wants the sheriff in a western to outdraw the

villain at high-noon on Main Street. They want Rocky to pummel Apollo Creed. They want Luke Skywalker and Darth Vader to battle it out with light sabers.

Anything less than a one-on-one showdown doesn't have the visual clarity and emotional power you want for the ending of a blockbuster movie.

Aliens

"Get away from her, you bitch!"
—*Aliens*

In the movie *Aliens*, the screenwriter James Cameron devised a triple whammy ending, using all the techniques we've just covered.

The story takes place on a space outpost that's been savagely decimated by the alien creatures. When Ripley, played by Sigourney Weaver, arrives with a small military team, the killing continues as the team is attacked by the unstoppable creatures.

Then they make a horrible discovery. There's a gigantic and monstrous Alien Queen who's hatching countless new offspring.

To kick up the intensity even more, there's also a "a ticking clock." The outpost is rigged to explode. So Ripley doesn't just have to defeat the monstrous Alien Queen . . . tick, tick, tick . . . SHE HAS TO DO IT NOW!

Needless to say, Ripley kicks serious Alien Queen butt and the audience loves every extra-strength blow. It's a happy ending as Ripley rockets away, leaving a planet-rattling fireball exploding in her wake. Then, at the exact moment when the audience lets their guard down, Cameron throws in his final unexpected surprise. The still-alive Alien Queen is on the ship. The story isn't over yet. *There's one more battle to go.* Despite the enormous difference in size, the climax is a face-to-face battle between Ripley and the Queen. Ripley jumps into a mechanical exo-skeleton that gives her the strength to go toe-to-alien-claw with the giant Alien Queen. It's the final audience-shocking surprise at the end of a great movie ride.

Blockbuster Three Act Structure is a dramatic tool to maximize the impact of your story. Its objective is to push you to give the audience an intense and soaring movie ride that excites their hearts, minds, and imaginations.

Your story may not use this structure completely. That's okay, too. Creating a new story may take you in a different direction. Just don't fall short of the overall goal that puts people in the seats.

Blockbuster screenplays are built to thrill.

Story Construction

As the following illustrates, screenwriters have lots of different ways for developing their initial movie idea into a story. Some will start writing with just a vague notion of where they want to go, while others prepare a much more detailed story map about what's going to happen at each step along the way. This process is personal for each writer.

But story structure is always an important overall objective. While some screenwriters may start writing with just a hazy idea, they know the end result has to be a terrific movie story with solid dramatic structure.

DAVID BENIOFF *(The 25th Hour)*

I want to know the beginning and the ending. I know the middle will work itself out as I'm writing. I have to know how it's going to end, because that's what I'm writing towards. Plus it's not as much fun if you write out too much beforehand, because part of the fun is creating that world and discovering it as you go.

Sometimes I do write a rough outline, I just tend not to study it too hard. I just find when I'm writing I ignore the outline, because I write one scene and it seems to me as I'm writing it I know what scene should come next. I'm not as organized as other screenwriters I know. I'm not saying that's a good thing. I'll end up writing seven drafts and maybe I could have saved myself some time if I'd been more organized.

PHILIP EISNER *(Event Horizon)*

I do an outline. It's usually about ten pages broken down into three acts. Structure is critical. You have to know where you're going. But you also have to allow your characters, especially in the first draft, to hijack the structure. You can't censor yourself, or let your preconceived notions restrict or stifle the story.

But after you finish the first draft, that's when you sit down and re-impose structure. Part of being a good writer is being a good editor. You have to be able to go back and look at your stuff and recognize what doesn't work.

AKIVA GOLDSMAN *(A Beautiful Mind)*

I always outline. I definitely break down the whole structure of the story, scene by scene, before I start writing. I used to do it on file cards, but now I do it on computer. I just list the scenes in a Three-Act Structure. I literally write the slug lines—INT. and EXT.—and I'll put a one-line sentence describing the scene. Sometimes I'll even put down some bits of dialogue if I have it. That's my map.

DAVID GOYER *(Blade)*

I write a beat outline. They tend to be ten to twenty pages per script. And I totally use Three Act structure.

I have to know fundamentally where I'm going. The few times I've tried to write a script without doing that, I've gotten completely lost midway. I write an outline, even if I end up diverging from it, because I think it's important to have some concept of where you're going and to be aware of the structure. It's the hardest part of writing though.

Before that I do research. When I do research, I have no

kind of editorial hat on at all. It's just a process of coming up with wild ideas and explorations and talking to experts. Then I dump it all into a file. It'll be ideas, snippets of dialogue, a little bit of everything. Then I'll start playing around with it and seeing if there's a kind of order that comes out of it. That's when I'll spend a couple of weeks working on my outline. Then I use that as my blueprint.

DAVID HAYTER (X-Men)

When I was first starting out, I said to myself, just keep it interesting, don't worry about structure. But what happens, if you've really studied movies like I have, is that your stories naturally fall into a classic Three Act structure.

You just fall into that rhythm without really thinking about it. I think that's important. Because if you try to force a story into structure without understanding why it works, it will come out awkward and stilted.

DALE LAUNER (My Cousin Vinny)

At writing seminars I used to say that I start with an outline, but it's a lie. I never started out with an outline. I couldn't for the life of me come up with an outline for a story and then write the screenplay from that outline.

I just start with an idea and spin off that idea. You keep rolling the dice and something else keeps coming up, and it snowballs. Snowballing is the best way to describe the evolution of the story. I'll usually come up with an outline somewhere along the way, but never in the beginning.

What I usually do is start with the kernel of an idea. The idea could be just a character in a situation, or a situation that will determine what the character will be.

ANDREW MARLOWE (Air Force One)

I find Three Act structure useful, but not in an aggressively formal sort of way. For me, having Three Act structure just means having a beginning, a middle, and an end.

I try to figure out where the story should start. Then I want to know where it will end. Once you have that, the whole process is getting your characters from that starting point to the end. It's creating that journey.

I then want to determine what is the process of personal growth for my main character, or what are the journey obstacles that have to be overcome. In an action movie, it's physical. What does the hero have to become? What situations does he have to get out of? Or it can be emotional if you have a character that starts out emotionally wounded. Then there will have to be specific events that will heal that emotional wound.

In the beginning, I'm going about my life, just thinking about it. I'm letting it steep in my mental tea cup. You let it ferment in your head for awhile. When you do that you get inspiration from all sorts of places as you go along.

Once I have a good sense of the idea, I'll write a treatment. I like to have some discovery in the writing process. If the outline is too specific, then I feel like I'm just coloring in the lines in a coloring book and I don't like that. The treatment is anywhere from five to ten pages.

SCOTT ROSENBERG *(Con Air)*

I always come up with an idea and I live with it for awhile. It's just in my head. I take it to bed. I take it to dinner. Then I immediately start thinking, who's in it? Who's the guy? Who's the girl? What's going on?

Then at a certain point I take out a legal pad and write one through sixty. Then I'll just start writing the scenes. It's a very loose outline, knowing where my Act One ends and my Act Two ends. Three-Act structure is really important. The great thing about the list is I check off the scenes as I go and I get a real feeling of accomplishment.

ED SOLOMON *(Men In Black)*

For me, every movie has its own rules for how it wants to be written. And these rules are not just unique movie to movie, they'll change within the movie, too. Some movies need to have detailed outlining all the way through. Others only need a detailed outline for part of it, and then part of it not. So I never say to myself that there's only one process of developing a story.

I push myself really hard when I'm trying to work something out, but I try to be extremely respectful of the internal workings of the piece itself. What does it need? Does the story need a very rigidly structured outline, or does it need to be more fluid?

I think people make a huge mistake in thinking that movies are just one thing. It's like saying a symphony needs something specific. It doesn't exist before it exists. Every story has a structure. It may or may not be a story with a Three-Act structure. Some movies have an organic, internal Three-Act structure. Others have a different structure. Structure is crucial, but it's a different structure for every story.

YOU HAVE TO WORK HARD AND PLAY HARD

"Use the force, Luke."
—Star Wars

The previous chapters have taken you through the preliminary stages of creating your story.

At this point, you've given your imagination time to wander and explore, you've done research to stimulate ideas, and you've finished the more structured work of arranging your story elements into a cohesive form with a beginning, middle, and end.

Now it's time to sit down and write.

This is an entirely different kind of activity, requiring equal parts determination, talent, and dogged hard work. In this chapter, we're going to go through the steps involved in writing the screenplay—not just any screenplay, of course, but a million dollar screenplay.

START WITH AN OUTLINE

At this point, you're ready to outline your story. Starting with an outline is especially important for beginning screenwriters, because the task of writing a full-length screenplay can be daunting. An outline serves as a roadmap that keeps you on-track—so you don't get lost or run out of ideas along the way. More often than not, when beginning screenwriters try to write a screenplay without an outline they run out of creative steam, or the resulting screenplay is sloppy and unfocused.

When you're outlining your story, there are several methods. There's no right way or wrong way. Like everything else, most screenwriters develop their own personalized system. All writers have a different creative process. So will you. You should always use the techniques and creative tools that are best suited to your talents.

Following are the common ways most screenwriters outline their story before writing the screenplay.

Treatment (also called a synopsis)

This is a prose description of your screenplay story written in the present tense. The form resembles a short story. A treatment usually breaks the story into Acts and can include some dialogue if it's helpful. The length can be anywhere from a couple of pages to much longer.

Step Outline (also called a beat outline)

A step outline achieves the same purpose but in a different form. Also broken out into Acts, the step outline lists the individual scenes or key events of the story from beginning to end.

128

The focus is more on the physical action of the story. A step outline specifies more clearly the individual scenes or story events.

Index Cards

This method is similar to a step outline. Each scene or story event is written on its own individual index card. When finished, the screenwriter has a stack of cards that outline the story from beginning to end. This method is different from the others, though, because it's only for personal use. It's not a document that can be used as part of the collaborative process.

The reason many screenwriters like this method is because of its flexibility. You can lay the cards along the floor, or tack them up on a bulletin board, and you're able to "visualize" the movie as you read from the first card to the last. Then you can easily move the index cards around until you discover the best pace and structure for the story.

Which of these methods you want to use, or even another one of your own devising, is up to you. The process is different for every screenwriter. That includes how detailed you want your outline to be before you start writing. Some screenwriters like to know their story almost completely before they begin, while others like to have a looser roadmap that leaves more room for discoveries along the way.

But whatever you select, it will help bring you to a very exciting place. You've created a blockbuster story that has all the dramatic richness and spectacle movie audiences love.

CHOOSE YOUR WRITING WEAPON

As a beginning screenwriter you also have to decide how you're going to face the creative battle of writing your screenplay. The days of scratching out a novel or a screenplay in longhand are gone. There may be a few screenwriters somewhere still doing it the old-fashioned way, which at this point also includes using a typewriter, but not very many.

Computers have invaded the world of Hollywood screenwriting and taken almost total control. The reason is obvious, especially to the blockbuster screenwriter. In the fast-moving, rewrite-driven atmosphere of high stakes moviemaking, anything that saves time and facilitates the process is something to be embraced.

For screenwriting, you just need a personal computer with a word processing program. There's no need to go upper-range or high-end. Any dependable Mac or PC will do fine. That's it. If you can't afford one, then that's a good reason to work hard at your writing and everything else. Having a computer will make the process easier.

But it won't make you a better writer.

This includes the various screenwriting software programs that are available. Currently, Final Draft and Movie Magic Screenwriter are the most popular.

Being a blockbuster screenwriter has nothing to do with hardware or software. You already have the most important and powerful creative tool and it's absolutely free. It's your head and your heart. Imagination, creativity, and talent are where great screenplays will always come from.

A computer and screenwriting software will give a high-tech boost to the physical process of writing, but not the creative process. A computer will help you do all the writing and revising tasks in a quicker and more efficient manner. They improve your editing abilities (cutting and pasting, saving, creating copies) significantly. The software programs all have shortcuts for formatting and other screenplay-specific functions. Using screenwriting software insures that your screenplay will have a professionally formatted look, which is critical when you're ready to market it.

A computer isn't absolutely essential, but it's becoming more so everyday if you want to be a working screenwriter.

As for the various screenwriting programs that are available, you have to decide if they fit your writing personality. They'll speed up and enhance the writing process, but they'll also take away some of your freedom to individualize how your screenplay looks on the page.

Screenwriting programs tend to give screenplays a standardized look that some writers don't like. They also take some work to learn, especially for you dreamy, creative types (you know who you are), but the end result can definitely be worthwhile.

In the beginning, do you need them to write a blockbuster screenplay? No, because you already have what you need. That's the desire to write a great screenplay.

WRITERS WRITE

"No matter where you go, there you are."
—The Adventures of Buckaroo Bonzai

You are what you do.

So if you want to be a blockbuster screenwriter, you have to become a person who writes blockbuster screenplays. This sounds like an obvious statement, but it's also the core of what the challenge ahead is all about. After you've come up with a big idea, and developed that idea into high-energy story with maximum entertainment potential, it's now time to write it.

You have to go someplace all by yourself and spend hours, days, weeks, and months working all alone to write a great screenplay.

At this stage, the creative process becomes much more focused and goal oriented. You start on page one and keeping writing until you get to the end.

Every day.

One page after the other.

You have to sit down and not give up until you've finished writing the best screenplay you possibly can.

If this is the first screenplay you've written, then this stage will probably have as many challenges and surprises as your blockbuster story. There will be moments of excitement, sudden ups and downs, twists and turns, and emotional revelations. There will also be periods when you think all is lost and you want to throw what you've written in the trash and never write again.

Snap out of it!

What all screenwriters learn to accept is how difficult the process is. If it was easy, anybody could do it. They can't. Just ask somebody in the movie industry who reads screenplays for a living.

Writing any kind of screenplay takes commitment and time, especially if your life is already filled up with a job, a family, or anything else. Then finding the time to write may seem like an impossible task.

But that's also part of becoming a blockbuster screenwriter. You already have a life, but it's not the life you want. So your challenge is like the challenges you've created for the characters in your story. You're being tested to see if you have what it takes.

Will it be easy?

Nope.

But it can be done, because lots of people before you have already done it. All successful screenwriters started out as complete unknowns before they built their careers. And every single one succeeded with the same basic tools you have. That's determination, hard work, and the resolve to use your talent to the fullest.

One of the better known examples of a screenwriter who passed this test is Ron Bass. Today he's one of the busiest and most successful screenwriters in Hollywood. Some of the movies he's written are *Rain Man, Entrapment, My Best Friend's Wedding,* and *What Dreams May Come.*

Screenwriting, though, is his second career.

Before that he was a top Hollywood entertainment lawyer, working long hours in a very tough and demanding job. But he'd always wanted to be a writer, so he started setting his alarm clock for 3 a.m. and writing until six. He'd put in a long day at the office, then wake up again the next morning at the same time and write. He was also a husband and father, which took time too. But finally, after enduring this grueling schedule, he was able to quit his day job and became a full-time screenwriter.

Why did he do something as crazy and difficult as waking up at 3 a.m. every day?

Because writers write.

CONTROL WHAT YOU CAN

You can never completely control the creative process. Sometimes it's running at full-power and the ideas are tumbling into your head faster than you can write them down, while other times you're ready and waiting, but nothing very good comes along.

That's why it's helpful to do whatever you can to inspire your creative energies.

All writers have different personalities and talents, so their creative process operates in different ways.

Make Your Writing Space Personal

Writing a screenplay is a combination of regimented hard work and imaginative play. It's both focused and uninhibited at the same time. You have to work very hard, but do so with a sense of fun and daring. You're like a marathon runner who isn't afraid to wander off the main road and explore for awhile.

Why? Because it's off the main road where unexpected moments of discovery happen. A new idea or twist suddenly pops into the writer's head and it makes the story better. No screenplay should ever go absolutely according to plan. Along the way, the writer should always be playing with ideas and trying new things, never allowing the creative door to close on his or her imagination.

As such, your writing space should accommodate the dual nature of the process. It should be a place where you can go everyday that's specifically for the purpose of writing. It's a work-place, so there shouldn't be any distractions or interruptions. Have everything you need to get the work done, from a dictionary and thesaurus to the necessary office supplies.

Most writers also like to personalize their writing space and make it a play space, too. It can be with music, art, movie posters, favorite books, toys, photographs, or anything else that connects a writer to their inner creative spirit. Writing is a very personal process, so the place where it's done should be personal, too.

Keep a Schedule

Another part of being a blockbuster screenwriter is simply getting it done. Top level screenwriters are paid the big bucks because they've proven they can deliver the goods. While the creative process has it's ups and downs, blockbuster screenwriters all have the talent and work ethic to do what they're paid to do, which is write a terrific screenplay and hand it in on time.

Like any other profession, being a screenwriter is a job, and you have to get the job done.

To do this, writing needs to be an essential and fundamental part of your everyday life. Even if it's not your job now, you should treat it like one. Having a writing schedule means writing every day. Weekends can be rest time, but only if you really need it. If you have a cold, it doesn't matter. Feeling tired and sluggish? That doesn't count either. If you want to be a blockbuster screenwriter, then you have to be determined and focused, because that's what it takes to participate at this level.

Your writing routine can be personalized, too. Everybody has their best time of day, whether it's in the morning, during the day, or even late at night. Schedule your writing around the period that works best for you.

Ultimately, the best writing schedule is to write as well as you can, as often as you can, for as long as you can.

The Goal Is To Finish

Another factor you want to control is your mental and emotional attitude while writing your screenplay.

What's key is to not put too much pressure on yourself to write the perfect screenplay.

This is a creative trap that some screenwriters get caught in. It happens when they put so much pressure on themselves that nothing they write seems good enough. They keep trying harder and harder, but it's a no-win situation. The writing often slows down to an agonizing crawl, as every word is put under a super critical microscope. The waste basket begins to overflow as the writer's spirits sink lower and lower.

More often than not, the screenwriter who falls into this trap won't keep writing. The creative process becomes too frustrating and painful, instead of challenging and fun.

Of course, you want to work hard and write as well as you can. Just remember that writing a screenplay is a process, and a big part of that process is revising and rewriting.

When you're writing your first draft, do the best you can, but also allow yourself the freedom to know you can go back whenever you want and make it better later. Don't spin your creative-wheels for too long at any one stage. Move on, keep up a steady pace, get to the end.

Screenwriters who obsess over every page like it contains the secret of the universe are forgetting the most important goal, which is finishing the screenplay. All screenwriters have great days, good days, and bad days. Successful screenwriters don't let their creative process get in the way of getting the job-done. They write to the finish line.

The bottom-line is: use what works.

If there's any part of your writing process that isn't helping you write in the most efficient, positive, and productive way possible, then it needs to be changed.

Writing a screenplay is demanding, so make your writing process as supportive as possible.

How We Do It

As we've just discussed, screenwriting is intensely psychological, but it's also mechanical. It's psychological because it involves digging into the deepest part of your personality and creativity. The mechanical part is the act of simply going somewhere every day and doing it.

In the following, the screenwriters talk about the writing process and reveal what works.

WRITING IS FUN, EXCEPT WHEN IT ISN'T

Most of the screenwriters love to write. They get a sense of almost giddy pleasure out of coming up with ideas and creating a story. That doesn't mean it's always easy, or there aren't times when the ideas don't come. But successful screenwriters learn to accept and understand the psychological nature of the process and work as effectively as they can.

DAVID BENIOFF *(The 25th Hour)*

I tend to write really late. I write from ten at night till three in the morning. It's not something I would recommend to other writers; it's just that I'm a procrastinator, especially in Los Angeles, where I always want to go out and run around. Eventually, it gets to be late at night and you realize you haven't written anything.

There is something about working at night. There's a different psychological mood. I don't set a page goal, but you kind of know when you've done a good day's work.

NEAL BRENNAN *(Half Baked)*

I love coming up with ideas. I love having an idea. It's an adrenaline rush, a real physical feeling of excitement. It's like knowing you're going to get laid that night. Because when you get the idea it's perfect. The problem is every stage after that gets messier.

PHILIP EISNER *(Event Horizon)*

I really enjoy writing. The only thing I can equate it to is golf. You're going to have days when you're terrible, and you're going to have days when you hit a fantastic drive.

Here's what I enjoy the most. When you're writing and

something comes to you. It may be a concept, or something about a character, or it may be as simple as finding the right word for a sentence. And you know, at that moment, that when the reader reads it, their head is going to snap back. That's why I love writing horror or action. I'm actually going for a visceral reaction from someone.

AKIVA GOLDSMAN (A Beautiful Mind)

After I've completed my outline, I try to write ten bad pages every day. I try to work a lot of hours, from early in the morning until the end of the day. I just want to knock something out. Sometimes I'll just write pieces of scenes. Stuff I can't figure out, I'll skip over and leave a note to myself. I don't agonize. Whatever comes out, comes out.

My goal is to get the story to lay down in a shape that's 120 pages or thereabouts. Then I can see where it needs work. I can see where it starts to bulge where it shouldn't, what needs to be worked out more or trimmed down. Then I start to rewrite.

But my psychological state when I start a screenplay is always the same. It's a mix of fear, anxiety and insecurity. Every script is the same. At some point when I'm writing, I always think I'm going to fail. That's not a joy. At this point, though, since it happens every time, I know it's not necessarily true.

DAVID HAYTER (X-Men)

When I first start to write I always find myself putting it off, because I'm afraid. It just seems so overwhelming. You know, sixty scenes that have to be great. All that dialogue, too. It's like an avalanche facing you and that's a little intimidating.

But I've gotten to the point where I don't have any fear that I will find my out. I know that I know what I'm doing, and I know the ideas will always be there. I think it's also an attitude. A lot of writers think if it's not hard, then it's not good. For me though, it's best when I find that place where my fingers are racing across the the keys, and I'm just delighted by how quickly and easily it's coming out, and how beautifully it's all coming together. At that point, I feel it's not even me anymore, it's the story taking on it's own life.

And you can't try to have everything be perfect when you're writing. Sometimes what's imperfect is what's interesting. You have to be willing to put out things that are skewed and have a good idea come later.

DALE LAUNER *(My Cousin Vinny)*

Writing is fun. There has to be a reason why people write and enjoy it. When you've created something, and you go back and look at it, and it's good, it's just a great high. It's fantastic.

When you get those big fat checks in the mail, that's nice, too. But it's really not as much fun as the writing.

ANDREW MARLOWE *(Air Force One)*

Writing well is really hard work. It's a process. I know there's an aspect of it I'm really good at. I'm very confident when I can see the moment in my head. When I start to watch the movie in my head like a giddy fan, then I know I have something.

When I can come up with something clever and fun in the middle of an action scene, it puts a smile on my face. I love that moment. Or when I'm in a dramatic scene and I come up with that one right line that makes everything work, it's an amazing feeling.

I try to write my first draft really quickly. I write the first draft with flaws and warts and zits. But you don't show that to anybody. That's just the document for you to edit. That's the slab of marble you're going to chisel.

SCOTT ROSENBERG *(Con Air)*

I'm extremely confident. When I sit down at the computer and it's going well, and most of the time it is, I'm a happy guy. When I'm into something and it's going well, there's no place I'd rather be.

I always knew it was going to happen. There was no back-up plan. I think it's the same with most really successful writers.

They just know they can do it. By the way, that doesn't preclude the times when you hand something in and they don't get it. Have there been disappointments? Of course.

I write fast. I've written twenty-five pages in a day. There's nobody faster than me when it's cooking. I can write a first draft in a week or two. And I always have very loud music blasting in the background. You have to remember, nobody's going to see your draft until you want them to.

ED SOLOMON (Men In Black)

I love writing. Some people don't like the blank page,but I love it. I think it's the greatest. It's like a ski slope before anybody has skied down it. It's beautiful. It's full of hope, potential, and possibility.

BLOCKBUSTER BRAINS CAN GET BLOCKED TOO

Because writing in so psychological, one of the job-related hazards is writer's block. It's when your inner creative mechanism develops a malfunction and stops running at full steam, or even running at all.

Here the screenwriters share their own personal techniques for beating writer's block. When it happens, the trick is to find a trick that works for you.

PHILIP EISNER (Event Horizon)

I just try to write through it and not worry if I'm writing crap or not. I just try to write anything, it doesn't have to be my story. I will write anything I feel like writing, but I have to fill a page. And it's keeping that habit going that helps me through whatever block I'm having.

AKIVA GOLDSMAN *(A Beautiful Mind)*

I don't believe in writer's block. Look, writing is a job. All writers have terrible days and terrible weeks and terrible sentences. But the only way to a good sentence is through a hundred bad ones. At least for me. If I was always waiting to write until I knew it would be good, I'd never write.

DAVID GOYER *(Blade)*

When I get really stuck, I'll stop writing for a week. Or what I'll do is, I won't write in sequence. I'll jump ahead and work on something I know I won't be stuck on. Also, occasionally, I'll write a preliminary draft that has some holes in it. Because you can always come back.

Sometimes, in my first draft, if I can't quite think of what I want to say in a scene, I just put what it has to be about, then come back later and put in the actual dialogue.

DALE LAUNER *(My Cousin Vinny)*

With creativity there are two personalities involved, the parent and the child. The child will sit down and just play, being purely creative. The other hat you put on is the parent or critic. The critic judges what you've done and decides whether it's good or bad. What happens when you get blocked is your parent or critic is too strong and negative.

If I find I'm blocked, it's usually because I'm a little depressed in my personal life. And if you're a little depressed, your inner critic is just going around knocking everything. So you have to go deal with that. Or what I've found is the critic is just getting too tough. I can't seem to write. Every time I go to write, the critic keeps saying, "That's no good . . . that's no good . . . ." You can't even get past the first sentence. Once I identify it, I acknowledge to myself that I'm being too tough on myself. So I know I have to go back to being playful. I just write and don't stop. Don't be afraid of where it's going to go. Once you do that and really let it go, pretty soon you're out there surfing the big wave again and it's big fun.

ANDREW MARLOWE *(Air Force One)*

There's no such thing as writer's block, only writer's embarrassment. It happens when you're embarrassed that you don't have the right idea to solve a story problem and you're embarrassed by the drivel you're starting to turn out. So you stop.

But if you press through and you're willing to solve the problem with the wrong solution, knowing it's wrong, you'll be able to write pages and pages. And suddenly, something will break through and you will be able to get to a moment that will help you solve whatever had you blocked. But the hardest part is getting over the sense that you're going to be wasting your time because all you're going to be writing is crap.

SCOTT ROSENBERG *(Con Air)*

I've only gotten writer's block a couple of times. I don't recommend it, but here's what I do.

If I'm writing a script and I'm slogging through the mud in the Second Act and I get stuck, I'll cancel all my plans for that Friday night. Then I'll go out and buy a whole bunch of beer. I'll put the beer in a cooler and I'll put the cooler next to my desk. I open the first beer and I start writing. I keep going and going. After about six or seven hours, I'm hammered. Absolutely drunk as a skunk. I go to bed. I wake up the next morning and read the pages. Eighty percent of it is absolute garbage. But twenty percent of it usually gets me through the problem I had. It freed me up.

ED SOLOMON *(Men in Black)*

I've found that writer's block usually comes from placing way too much importance on the one idea that's going to be your magnum opus, that's going to make or break your entire future forever, for the rest of history. When I'm stuck, there are two methods that, for me, are fool-proof.

The first is I'll write about what I'm writing. Literally, I will write, "Now I am having trouble writing this sequence where I know this has to happen but I don't know, how." And gradually, just the process of articulating it opens it up.

I also believe wholeheartedly in the power of the unconscious to do a lot of the heavy lifting. So I'll often stop writing if I'm having trouble. Because I know myself enough to know that there are days when nothing is going to happen. For whatever reason, it's just not happening and I know it. On those days I will actively take the day off. And I'll consciously give myself an assignment, which is that when I come back tomorrow, I want to have worked out the problem I'm having with the script.

More often than not, when I come back my subconscious has solved the problem.

THE WRITE PLACE

Screenwriting is a job, so you need to develop a daily routine that's both productive and effective. Your writing time and space should be protected as an essential part of your day.

While the screenwriters interviewed all have a slightly different writing process, they all have a schedule and a place to write that's creatively nurturing. Some set page goals and others don't. But the objective is always to develop a writing process that works.

NEAL BRENNAN *(Half Baked)*

I work in my apartment. A normal day is, I wake up around eleven o'clock. A couple of days a week, I go to therapy. I'll come home, drink coffee, eat, and start writing around two-thirty or three. An average day is four pages. I get that in about three hours. I use Final Draft screenwriting software. But as any writer knows, you're always writing in your head. You're always working.

If I'm writing with a partner, it's always in the same room. We outline together and write the script together. We discuss a scene, or idea, then one person types. We keep going over it until it's right.

PHILIP EISNER *(Event Horizon)*

I take my laptop into my wife's office in our house. Or I go to the public library. I have an office at home with all my stuff in it, but I can't write there. It's a great place to come up with ideas, but that's it. Because if I'm stuck I'll start playing around, or start surfing the Internet. I have to be in a place where I'm not distracted.

AKIVA GOLDSMAN *(A Beautiful Mind)*

I write in my house. Wherever I'm living, I always have a little office. And I need to be able to see far away. I have to have a window. It's really hard for me to write without one. And I need to be able to see a piece of sky.

I need to be able to stare out into the distance with no barriers. I have no idea why, it's just important to me. I go all day long. I try not to write at night, and I try not to write on weekends.

DAVID GOYER *(Blade)*

I write in my office, or I'll go away and ensconce myself in some quiet hotel somewhere. Most of my last scripts have been written that way. I can write for about four or five hours, then my brain explodes.

I'll get a first draft, then I'll go back and do a little bit of trimming. Then, if I can afford it, I'll put it in a drawer for two to four weeks to get some distance on it. Then I come back and put on my editorial hat. Whatever the studio sees is usually the second draft.

DAVID HAYTER *(X-Men)*

I write in an office. But basically, like Stephen King says, all you need is a locked door, a place where you're not bothered by anybody. When I'm in full writing mode, I'll come in and do eight hours a day and do eight pages. That's when I'm really rolling and all I'm doing is writing.

JIM KOUF *(Rush Hour)*

I'm in my office from nine to five everyday. And I'm writing, or at least I'm trying to. My goal is five pages every day. On a really good day I can do ten pages.

Paying the bills is the best inspiration I know.

DALE LAUNER *(My Cousin Vinny)*

I write at home, and I try to write every day. I try to set myself a page count every day. If it's rewriting, though, it's different. I enjoy it and I don't know how to stop.

ANDREW MARLOWE *(Air Force One)*

I write in my office in Santa Monica and at home. When I'm in production, I hire an assistant for the outer reception area. In the inner office, I have a desk with all my stuff. I write on a portable computer that I use at home, too. I have a TV to watch movies and file cabinets. I'm generally surrounded by piles of paper, whether it's previous drafts, or what I'm working on.

I get in around ten o'clock and work until four-thirty or five. My day depends on where I am in the writing process. If I'm starting out and there's a lot of think work, I'll come in around ten and screw around for about an hour of so. I'm thinking in my head. I'll go out for a walk, get coffee, read the paper. It looks like I'm doing nothing. But I'm thinking, working through stuff.

You're doing it consciously and subconsciously.

Then things start to come into focus. I start to hit the pages. Then I'll work more and more aggressively and more and more intensely as the process goes on. Finally, I'll get so deep into it I won't even bother going to the office. I'll just get out of bed and go to my workspace at home and start working. I'll look up and eight hours have gone by. It's like a snowball rolling down a hill. The last two weeks I shut everything else out and I'm totally living in the story.

SCOTT ROSENBERG *(Con Air)*

I try not to write in Los Angeles. It's always sunny and seventy and there's lots to do. So I tend to do most of my work on the East Coast. I use Final Draft. I work in my apartment.

When I really truly need to work and I'm up against a deadline, I go to Boston where I grew up, and I go to my mother's house. It's the best, because it's rainy and cold, and all my friends are married with kids, so they don't bother me. I wake up, my mom brings me coffee, and I write.

ED SOLOMON *(Men in Black)*

I usually write in my office. It's on a little street in Santa Monica above a shoe store. The front room is empty, and I sometimes use it as an exercise room. The back room is like a giant living room. I have a big plasma TV screen to watch films on if I need to. Two of the walls are completely covered with dry erase white boards that are metallic. I like them being metallic because I can use magnets and move things around. I can also write on them. I have big-size pens and small-size pens. I can use the small pens to write dialogue and the big pens to write concepts. That's usually how I outline a movie, on these big boards with different sized pens.

I go there in the morning after dropping my son off at school. I'll usually try to sit silently for about half an hour to gather my thoughts. Then I might go down to the coffee shop and sit for an hour or two with a notepad and think about what I'm going to write during the day. Then I go back to the office and write. I try not to have lunch. I find it uses up too much energy and cuts into the middle of writing time. I tend to write through lunch until late afternoon. I used to listen to music a lot before I'd write, because it put me into an emotional mood. I always find it easier to write from an emotional place than an intellectual place.

BLOCKBUSTER WRITING STYLE

*"I feel the need, the
need for speed."*
—Top Gun

As a blockbuster screenwriter, you should also never forget that you're a performer. You're just like an actor, a singer, or a magician performing tricks for a wide-eyed audience.

The only difference is the page is your stage. As a screenwriter you're every bit as entertainment driven as any other performer. You're performing for the reader. When you're writing your screenplay, you want to sell your movie on the page to the reader.

You do that with writing style.

You do it with words that tell the story in the most exciting and vivid way possible. When the reader opens your script and reads "FADE IN" the performance begins.

As we've said all along, there's nothing modest or meek

about a blockbuster movie. That includes the way the screenplay is written. The best blockbuster screenplays entertain readers and leaves them breathless, as if they've just stumbled out of a real life movie theater. From the first page to the last, readers should see and feel the story on that private movie screen in their heads.

SCREENPLAY FORMAT

Screenplay format is the standardized way in which screenplays are written, and learning this format is essential. Everything about your screenplay should say "this is the work of a skilled professional," and nothing says that quicker than using proper format.

If you've decided to use a screenwriting program, then the job is done. If you don't know format, then the most comprehensive guide is *The Complete Guide to Standard Script Formats: The Screenplay* by Cole/Haag.

If your screenplay has sloppy or incorrect format, it will usually prompt an industry reader to stop reading and toss it in the reject pile. If you haven't bothered to learn the most basic part of screenwriting, you'll be judged as a wanna-be amateur.

GET INSIDE THEIR HEADS

Along with using correct format, you also want to develop a writing style that's as compelling and engaging as the movies you want to write. Remember, you're performing on the page for the reader. Blockbuster screenwriters use language to maximize the impact of their stories for the reader. The most effective blockbuster writing style reads like poetry on steroids.

It's concise.
It has momentum.
It's clear and descriptive.
It's entertaining to read.

Most of all, readers should feel as if they're watching a movie. That's the key. Whatever kind of story you're writing, readers must experience the sensations as though they're seeing the movie right before their eyes.

If it's a comedy, they should be laughing. If it's a horror story, they have to be goose-bumpy and scared as they're turning the pages. If it's an action-adventure story, they should feel the same heat-thumping excitement and exhilaration they would feel if they were sitting in the movie theater.

You want whoever reads your screenplay to think, "THAT'S A GREAT MOVIE!"

Writing style is how you communicate your movie vision to the reader.

Be Concise

This means not overwriting. The goal in writing your screenplay is always to be precise, not long-winded.

Some beginning screenwriters think if they describe a scene as accurately as they can it gives more reality to the story. They'll describe what a character is wearing, what kind of shoes, what color socks, whether the shoe laces are tied. On and on and on. But all that isn't important to the story.

In blockbuster screenwriting, the goal is to use sharp and concise language instead of long, overly detailed descriptions of the location, characters, and action.

Here's one way to describe the location, characters and action in a scene:

EXT — CITY - MIDNIGHT

A full moon peeks out from behind silvery clouds that hang quietly in a black night sky.

It's midnight.

We're in a bad part of town. The tenement buildings and dilapidated storefronts are all covered with dirt and grime. Neon blinks in a bar window. A drunk screams into a broken pay phone. Lots of broken dreams end up here.

A WAILING police siren is heard.

TWO MEN

Stroll out of a dark alley. They're dressed in urban grunge. Jeans, ripped t-shirts, stubble beards. Probably late twenties. One has red curly hair. The other has a baseball cap pulled low. They look like they've just met in a police line-up. They walk slowly, whispering, eyes darting around.

Not bad, but here's a better way:

EXT - CITY - MIDNIGHT

The crummy part of town.

TWO LOW-LIFES in their twenties slither out of a dark alley. They're bad boys on the prowl.

The best screenwriting style communicates the dramatic essence of a scene without resorting to an overly detailed description of all the specific elements.

One reason this isn't necessary is because all these tiny details are rarely translated to the screen. When the movie-making machine starts rolling, the director, the casting agent, the set designer, the wardrobe department, and all the other production participants make these choices.

Another reason you want to be concise is because screenplays are relatively short. While novels can be hundreds of pages, a screenplay is rarely more than 120 pages. When you're writing a blockbuster story with that page limitation, you want every word to count. Just tell the story, don't describe every little detail. Be crisp and to the point.

Momentum Keeps Your Screenplay Moving

While writing style communicates your movie vision, the script has to move at a good pace to carry to reader along with it. Momentum keeps your movie thrill ride up to speed.

Being concise is one of the ways you do that. Keep your descriptive paragraphs short. Long paragraphs slow the reader down and slow the story, too. Ideally, the screenplay should move at the same pace as the movie. You want the readers to be seeing the movie in their heads. Anything that's overwritten or sluggish on the page puts the movie in a reader's head in slow-motion too.

Momentum also means not breaking the mood of the story. The best blockbuster screenplays pull the readers into the world of the story and keep them there until the final fade-out. Anything that takes a reader out of this imaginative world breaks the mood.

Lots of camera directions will do this. Some beginning screenwriters love to use camera directions, because they think it makes their screenplay look professional. Not true. They cut directly into the suspension of disbelief you want from the reader. Every camera direction is a visual intrusion that will remind readers that they're reading a screenplay. You want the reader lost in the world of your story, and you can't accomplish this with camera directions that are constantly reminding them they're reading a screenplay.

Plus, it's a mistake to think it's your job as a screenwriter to direct the way the movie should be shot. Only use camera directions (CLOSE UP:, DISSOLVE:, POV, etc.) when absolutely necessary. If you can, it's always better to use regular language to achieve the same effect.

Here's one way to describe the action in a scene:

INT - BEDROOM - NIGHT

A 16-YEAR-OLD GIRL lies on her bed, flipping though a photograph album.

CLOSE-UP: THE ALBUM

There's a picture of a young boy sitting
in front of a birthday cake.

CLOSE-UP: HER FACE

Tears well in her eyes when she sees the picture.

BACK TO SCENE

She closes the book, and more tears come as she remembers her younger brother, who was killed in a car accident.

Here's a better way:

INT - BEDROOM - NIGHT

A 16-YEAR-OLD girl lies on her bed, flipping through a photograph album.

She stops at a picture. Tears come to her eyes. It's a young boy in front of a birthday cake.

She closes the book, and now more tears come as she remembers her younger brother, who was killed in a car accident.

The camera directions in the first version break the mood of the scene and aren't necessary. In the second version, it's still indicated you need a close-up of the picture and another close-up to see the girl's tears. It's the director's job to shoot the scene in a way that visually communicates this information. It's your job to write a screenplay that tells "the story."

Momentum is a combination of writing style and story construction. It's writing the screenplay in a way that keeps the reader turning the pages faster and faster until they get to the end. Momentum is also about having a great story, so the pages are worth turning.

Be Clear and Descriptive

When you're writing your screenplay avoid anything vague. That is one of the deadly sins of blockbuster screenwriting, along with boring, wimpy, and snoozy.

A blockbuster story can be filled with mysteries and puzzles, but the writing style shouldn't be. Tell your story in commonly used language that's easily understandable. No arcane or obscure words. No overly used jargon or expressions that are too specialized or technical.

You're writing a blockbuster movie for a mainstream audience, so make sure your screenplay is accessible to a broad audience, too.

Descriptive language is how you paint your movie vision on the page. Write with sharp language that avoids cliché but is easily understandable to the reader.

Your screenplay should be reader-friendly. That means it should be fun to read, not an eye-straining chore. If the reader has to fight their way though page after page of overwritten and vague storytelling, this will also put the brakes on your story momentum.

Write with Your Personal Voice

Having a strong "writing voice" will also enhance your screenplay's appeal and effectiveness.

Think about it this way. Imagine you're at a party and someone walks over and begins to tell you a story. You listen carefully but you notice the person's voice is very soft. They also stand very still and the words come out without any kind of emotional force or conviction. They get to the end of the story without once changing their expression. They also mumbled and stared at their feet.

Then a second person walks over and tells the same story. But this person puts their whole body and soul into it. Their voice rises and falls with every dramatic twist and turn. Their body tenses with anger, then shakes with laughter, then tears come when they slowly describe a heartbreaking event. By the end, it turns out you've been laughing and crying right along with them.

The second is obviously better, right?

That's because the story is told in a "voice" that sells every dramatic moment of the story.

Voice" is using your personality on the page. It's writing your screenplay with all the power and persuasion you have. We all see the world differently and that's where your voice comes from. A writer's voice is like a dramatic fingerprint. It's what makes your story special and unique. If you think of the top-selling novelists, they all have a very specific voice: Stephen King. Tom Clancy. Ann Rice.

Blockbuster screenwriters have distinctive voices, too.

Shane Black (*Lethal Weapon*, *Long Kiss Goodnight*) is known for his super-charged action writing style and funny, tough-guy jokes to the reader. William Goldman (*Marathon Man*, *Princess Bride*) is known for his relentlessly visual and vivid way of writing his screenplays. Robert Towne (*Chinatown*, *Days of Thunder*) writes with an energy and sense of character that's always pitch perfect.

But your writing voice also has to match the story you're

telling. The voice and writing style should always serve the story, not overwhelm or detract from it. If you're writing a high-tech action movie, one kind of voice is called for. If you're writing a historical romance, a different voice is required.

All the screenwriters in this book have great writing voices, too. They're all different and personal, but for all of them, it's one of the reasons they're successful screenwriters. How they sell their story on the page is one of the reasons they're able to sell their screenplays for big paychecks.

A GREAT WRITING STYLE MAKES YOU UNIQUE

For the beginning screenwriter, your writing style has the potential to make your screenplay stand out from all the others that are trying to get noticed, too. Your screenplay has to pass through a gauntlet of tough-minded readers who have to love it, so yours must be different and special.

You can do that with a voice and a writing style that's as new and exciting as the blockbuster story you're telling. It's a Hollywood refrain you hear time and time again. Everybody in the movie business is always looking for writers with a "new and original voice."

Here's what you already know: Right now, there's nobody writing with your voice, because nobody's lived your life. If you want to be blockbuster screenwriter, then one of the ways you can do it is to give the movie industry what they want. A unique voice.

Writing Style

Blockbuster screenwriters understand the importance of developing a strong and effective writing style. Most consciously craft the language to communicate their movie story in the most emotionally charged and exciting way possible.

At the same time, all the interviewed screenwriters stressed the need for clarity and concision. In blockbuster screenplays, you want to pack the biggest punch you can into the fewest, well-chosen words.

DAVID BENIOFF *(The 25th Hour)*

The screenplay is obviously just a blueprint, a step in the process. That said, when you're trying to sell it, you're trying to get people to buy a story. Obviously, the more they like the story, the better your chances of selling it. So the actual writing of the screenplay is very important.

A lot of times, with beginning screenwriters, it seems like the stage directions are sloppy, the grammar's atrocious, and they haven't even spell-checked. That stuff makes a difference. You need every advantage you can get. There are so many hundreds of thousands of screenplays out there—anything you can do that puts you above the herd is helpful. You have to try really hard to write a screenplay that's enjoyable to read.

I think the writing style should match the tone of the story. I think the objective is always to bring the reader into a world, create that willing suspension of disbelief.

You don't want to ever have a line that detracts the reader from that goal.

Also, pay very close attention to where the scenes should end from a technical standpoint. Young screenwriters often tend to have their scenes go on for too long. They tend to drift past the point where it's dramatically interesting. I also think it's critical to know how one scene plays into the next.

PHILIP EISNER *(Event Horizon)*

I think the short story classes I took in college were really helpful. There's a very specific style in short stories that works very well in a screenplay. You have to always be on-track with the story, and you can't be frivolous with language. I write science-fiction, where you have to describe a world in your screenplay. In a screenplay you don't have the time to describe everything in detail. You've got to pick a few things that will completely ground that environment for the reader, then keep the story moving.

A lot of people criticize Shane Black and other writers who use witty asides to the reader. But you do that because you just really want the reader to get it.

That's actually the most fun part of the craft, the tricks. It's when you're confident enough in your own writing and in your ability to tell the story that you can then reach into your bag of tricks for specific story purposes. At a particular moment you ask yourself, what can I do to shock the reader? This is a moment the reader needs to be scared. What can I do to scare the reader, or make it really clear that even if the reader isn't scared, the audience will be?

Pace is extremely important in a story, and it's something writers can control with white space. I use a lot of white space to propel the readers' eyes, so they read fast and keep turning the page to find out what happens next. I think there's nothing worse than a dense block of text. It also translates onto the screen, because everybody who's been reading the script has gotten the feeling that this movie moves fast.

For a screenplay, the experience takes place in the reader's head, so it's very important for the screenwriter to have an effective writing style. You need to develop a writing style that makes people actually look forward to reading your work. It's a great thing when somebody reads your work and says, "This isn't the movie we want to make right now, but we want to work with this writer."

AKIVA GOLDSMAN (A Beautiful Mind)

In screenwriting, the writer is the narrator of the story, and you become a kind of invisible character, too. So you want to make a personal connection with the reader, just like the characters in your story do. It's important that your writing voice reaches out and connects with the reader. I read my stuff over and over again, and I'm always trying to maximize emotional content and connectedness to the reader.

DAVID GOYER (Blade)

Beginning screenwriters tend to overwrite. They'll use overly florid descriptions. I'm constantly going through my scripts to see what I can trim down. The goal is to make them as lean as possible.

That said, you also want to write something that's enjoyable to read. In some cases, if you're coming up with whole new worlds, new concepts and creatures, you have to write enough so those that images jump off the page. But I still go through and trim things when I can.

I try to tailor my writing style to the material. My Blade scripts tend to be a little more over-the-top, a little crazier, a little more irreverent, because that's the kind of movie it is. It helps set the tone for the executives that are reading it.

I try to lay out the action beats very clearly. I try to visually build on the page a sense of momentum and escalating action that's exciting.

You have to be conscious of the reader. You're doing two things. You're providing a blueprint for the movie, but you're also writing a screenplay that, in all likelihood, is going to be read by an overworked, overburdened lower development executive, who lugs home a bag of ten screenplays and is just waiting for the opportunity to toss yours aside.

So never have chunks of unbroken long paragraphs of description. As a reader, they just don't even want to wade into it, it's so dense. I tend to never have any paragraphs longer than four lines. Just break those long paragraphs up. Make it easier for the reader.

DAVID HAYTER *(X-Men)*

What's important in screenwriting is the economy of the word. If your script starts getting much over 120 pages, the studio gets nervous, so you can't really take the time to be overly descriptive. In screenwriting you have to be powerful and concise with your language.

Simplicity and clarity are the most important. I just try to put myself in the world of the story, watch what's going on, then write it down for everybody else.

JIM KOUF *(Rush Hour)*

My writing style is to go for story clarity. I want to tell the story in the best way possible. I don't crack any jokes that won't be on the screen. When your screenplay is being read by someone who has to read ten other scripts that weekend, you just want to tell the story as well as you can.

DALE LAUNER *(My Cousin Vinny)*

I write as cleanly, and as simply as I can, with as few words as possible. I'll actually go through my script and do a word count. I want my scripts to be dense, but quick and fast. I don't write like a nineteenth century novelist. I use full sentences, but some writers don't. I want my scripts to be a really brisk read, like a good short story.

ANDREW MARLOWE *(Air Force One)*

What I'm trying to do is capture what I see in the movie that's playing in my head in the most concise and effective way I can. I don't use long blocks of text, because when the camera in my head moves to a new visual, I'm writing a new paragraph. When people read my screenplays, I want them to be seeing a movie, not thinking about how they'll be able to translate what I'm writing into a film.

SCOTT ROSENBERG *(Con Air)*

It's such a mistake to have giant blocks of text. I will never go more than four lines without breaking it up. When you open a page and see a really long paragraph you know it's a rookie screenwriter.

You have to remember, the people you want to read it—agents, producers, directors—have to read countless scripts. So make it fun for them, make it fast, make it a good time. Keep the descriptions to a minimum. Use language that's entertaining and sets the tone for the story.

ED SOLOMON *(Men in Black)*

I don't consciously make my scripts entertaining to read. If a script is well written, it's a good reading experience. I think all that self-conscious stuff just seems to me like desperate self-conscious stuff. If you're in control, then you're fine. Trust the story. Just trust the story. How is the story wanting to be told? Just tell it as simply and clearly as possible.

THE BULLET-PROOF SCREENPLAY

*"What are you trying to tell me,
that I can dodge bullets?*

*No, Neo. I'm trying to tell you that when
you're ready you won't have to."*
—The Matrix

Nothing is easy in the movie business.

It's difficult to get movies made, and it's equally difficult to break in and build a career.

It doesn't matter if you want to be an agent, an actor, a director, or any other key player. It takes talent and relentless, sometimes life-challenging determination.

If you're a beginning screenwriter, and you've just finished your first screenplay (or your second, or third), you probably already know it will be a big challenge to get the necessary people to read it. But you also know that's what you have to do in order to make your dream come true. Blockbuster screenwriters are dreamers and fighters.

So now the challenge is to get your screenplay to the right people who will make that dream come true.

Right?

Wrong.

Not just yet.

Because it's not the agent who's going to end up selling your screenplay. What everybody in the movie business knows is that there's really only one all-important force that will get your screenplay sold.

YOUR SCREENPLAY SHOULD SELL ITSELF

If you've written a truly terrific screenplay it will sell itself. Sure, you've got to work hard to get it read, but a terrific screenplay, will sell for a very simple reason. That's what everybody is looking for.

But your screenplay has to be ready for the fight ahead.

When you're sending it out to the marketplace, whether it's to an agent or anybody else, your screenplay has a very specific mission. It has to survive in a rough-and-tumble, high-stakes competition in which only the very best succeed. If your screenplay is weak or ineffective in any way, it will almost certainly be shot down.

So if you want your dream to come true, you have to prepare your screenplay for battle. Before sending it out to the marketplace, you have to make sure it has what it takes to survive and be a winner.

HOW TO MAKE YOUR SCREENPLAY BULLET-PROOF

Finishing a screenplay is always exciting. You've worked hard and created a movie story you love. But don't make the mistake of immediately rushing your screenplay out before it's truly ready.

Use the following check-list to make sure your screenplay has the blockbuster strength and power it will need for the battle ahead.

There's a Big Idea

First look and make sure your screenplay is built on a new and imaginative big idea. Does it send the characters and the action exploding off in exciting and unexpected ways.

The best blockbuster ideas bring something new to "the world of stories" and something new to "the world itself." It's a different way of looking at, revealing, or answering a big question. Does your screenplay reach for something big dramatically and do it in a big way?

Is your big idea capable of hooking an audience?

Is there something about it the audience will find fascinating, amazing, entertaining, mystifying, uplifting? Does it provoke a feeling that will motivate people to see the movie.

• How will your concept look on a movie poster?

• Will millions of people see the poster and want to see the movie?

You Maximized Your Big Idea

Whatever movie idea you started with, make sure you dramatized it in a story that fully realizes it's blockbuster potential. Be
certain that your screenplay pushes and energizes every element
in the story to it's highest level of intensity.

- Can the story be tighter, leaner, faster?

- Can the story be smarter, more entertaining?

- Is there a bigger, bolder, better way to visualize the story, or
  any of its parts?

- Does it have a range of story elements that will appeal to a broad
  audience—drama, action, humor, suspense, joy, surprise, recognition, revelation, transformation, transcendence?

- Is every element in the story fresh and new? Are there clichés,
  borrowed ideas, or any overly familiar story devices the audience has already seen before?

- Is every dramatic element in the story serving the story and
  the audience? Every moment in your screenplay has to keep
  the story moving and the audience not moving. If there's anything in your screenplay that's only there because it's personal
  and private, it doesn't belong.

The Story Is Emotionally Moving

Just because you've written a story with a big idea, doesn't make
it a blockbuster movie. It has to have a big heart, too.

Does your screenplay connect with the audience in a deep
and personal way? Remember, if your story is just filled with
mindless action and special effects, it won't connect strongly

with an audience. It might be exciting and fun to watch, but it will also be easily forgotten.

The audience has to care about your story and be emotionally invested for it to have dramatic power and resonance.

Go through your screenplay and make sure the characters have depth and complexity. Cartoonish or bland characters don't resonate with an audience. Be certain that the character's conflicts are as vivid and powerful as they can be. Nothing tugs at the emotions of the audience more intensely than believable characters struggling against overwhelming forces.

• Does the story touch the audience's emotions?

The Audience Connects with the Main Character

Take a hard look at your main character and see if he or she has the personality and qualities that will appeal to a broad audience. Is there a believable mix of flaws and strengths?

At the beginning of the story, your main character has to be different, troubled, searching, unhappy, unfulfilled, misguided, or unfairly treated in some way. The audience relates to these problems and inner dramatic wants. They feel a sympathetic and personal connection.

The character's strengths are also important. The audience then connects with the main character's desire to overcome and win. Your main character has to be strong, courageous, cool, idealistic, brave, unique, talented, resourceful, or gifted in some way. These qualities give the audience confidence in the character and allow them to vicariously experience the excitement of saving the day.

Finally, remember that blockbuster movies are big-screen rides with soaring highs and deep lows.

• Has your main character experienced both during the course of your screenplay?

It Understands The Genre

If you've written a genre movie, make sure the story delivers at the highest level of audience expectation.

A science-fiction movie has to be cosmically adventurous and intellectually challenging. A political thriller has to investigate, or stumble upon, the darker and sinister machinations of politicians and government. In every genre movie, there are unique and specific story elements that are essential.

As a blockbuster screenwriter, you have to give the audience what they want, then you have to give them more. In a blockbuster genre screenplay, you also want to break through the traditional expectations and give the audience something new—while making sure it satisfies genre expectations.

• Does your screenplay break through the clichés and formulaic boundaries the audience has become used to?

The Story Has Spectacle and Scope

Spectacle adds visual flash and sizzle to your story. Blockbuster movies always take the audience to exotic places they've never been before, or they show them exotic sights in places they thought they knew, but really didn't.

In the movie *E.T.*, most of the story took place in very normal surroundings: a suburban house. The local neighborhood. The school. The woods. Now think about your favorite scenes in the movie. I'll bet one of them is when Elliott and E.T. are being chased on the street ... and their bike suddenly flies up into the air and they soar over the treetops in front of the moon.

That's spectacle.

Go through your screenplay and make sure it has spectacle. Just like you want your characters to have complexity and depth to make them compelling, you want the visual personality of your movie to have spectacle so it's compelling, too.

Scope means your movie has size and ambition. It's about something that's big and important. Blockbuster movies reach high and far, even if they're about seemingly normal occurrences.

As you read over your screenplay, ask yourself if you've created a world in your screenplay that's big enough and complex enough to entertain millions of people. Audiences go to the movies to see new sights and experience new sensations.

• Does your screenplay provide spectacle and scope?

The Story Has Something to Say

Another key element you want in your screenplay is a dramatic and powerful theme.

One of the reasons stories are so important in our lives is because they give us something more than just passing entertainment. They also enrich, educate, guide, and inspire us. Audiences are always attracted to stories that have a strong point of view about life and how to live it.

Blockbuster movies are no different.

Make sure your screenplay has something to say about the human condition. The theme usually comes out of the main character's struggle and what he or she learns.

You obviously want your blockbuster screenplay to be entertaining and exciting, but it also has to have a theme that makes the story meaningful to the audience's lives. If it doesn't, then the story is just pictures and noise without anything to say.

• Does your screenplay have a strong theme that is meaningful to a big audience?

The Story Has Solid Craft and Structure

Make sure your screenplay is solidly constructed. This means going back over all the story elements and double-checking to see if they're effectively handled. It's like an architect going in and inspecting the inner structure of a house. No matter how beautiful and glorious the outer façade, the inner frame and foundation have to be strong. If they aren't, then problems are bound to occur.

It's the same with your blockbuster screenplay.

- Look at your Three-Act structure again. Does each Act do what it's supposed to do? Are the acts the right length? Is any part of the story unclear or confusing?

- Think about your characters, too. Are they the right characters to tell this story? Do the characters create the story? Does the story create changes in the characters?

- How's the dialogue? Does it fit the overall tone of the movie? Is it worthy of being spoken on a giant screen to millions of people?

- Does your screenplay have all the story elements audiences love—emotion, surprises, revelations, fights, struggles, failures, achievements?

- Does it also have an ending that rocks and rolls?

Evaluate Your Writing Style

Review your writing style. Can it be tightened, made clearer, more visual? Is it reader-friendly? Does it communicate the same sights and sensations to the reader that they'd experience watching the movie?

• Does every word on every page sell your movie story to the reader?

Get Feedback

Almost all professional screenwriters have trusted readers they give their screenplays to before officially releasing them from the inner sanctum of their writing room.

It's a necessary part of the process, because no matter how hard you've worked, you still need to hear what other people think. When you give your screenplay to a reader or readers you want them to give their opinion about the story, especially what they didn't like or understand. You want to hear about anything that will help you make the screenplay better.

You also want to hear what they liked and loved, because that's helpful, too. Any kind of storytelling is based on communicating with an audience, so you want to know from your readers if what you wrote communicated in the way you wanted it to.

What you want most from your readers is honesty.

Only use readers who will be straight-forward and honest with their opinions. This doesn't mean they have to go after the screenplay and the writer like a rabid dog, ripping and chewing and maiming until there's nothing left but a few scraps of paper and a devastated, broken-hearted screenwriter. Good readers know how to criticize in a way that's constructive and helpful, not mean-spirited and soul-crushing.

But you also don't want a reader who will only tell you how brilliant the screenplay is and how wonderful you are. That's not helpful either. It's fun, but not helpful. So it's usually not a good idea to give your screenplay to a mother, husband, or girlfriend. Not always, but usually, their feedback will be biased, and even if it isn't, you'll probably think it is.

The best readers are usually other writers, because they understand the creative process. They understand it's very much . . . *a process*. The writer is constantly trying new ideas, then revising and rewriting until the story is the best it can be.

Feedback is one of the ways you do that.

Even better is to have a group of readers who have different points-of-view. Of course, joining a writing group can accomplish this within a more structured framework. Readers will give you a clearer sense of how your story appeals to an audience. Everybody has a wide range of cinematic likes and dislikes in stories, so you want to hear from a variety of readers. That way, you'll be better able to identify the real problems in your screenplay from the criticism that's mostly personal and not as valid.

When you get back all the feedback from your readers, you need to consider it very carefully and thoughtfully. Most writers feel very protective of their writing and sometimes find it difficult to make changes. Don't fall into this trap. Care about your screenplay, not your ego. Never slavishly follow the feedback, or disregard it either. Only use what you think will improve your screenplay.

The process of getting feedback and revising should last until you honestly believe you've written the best screenplay you can.

• Did you assemble a varied group of readers to give you feedback on your screenplay?

• Did you honestly consider what they said and not let ego, pride or laziness stop you from using their feedback to make the screenplay better?

Final Proofread

After you've gone through the steps above, read your screenplay one last time and double check all the details. Is the format correct? Are there any misspellings or grammatical errors? Any missing pages? Is the printing quality excellent?

• Check it again. Be absolutely sure.

Protect Your Work

Finally, remember to always protect the originality of your screenplay by registering it with the Writer's Guild. You can do it in person, call for a registration form, or register online. The fee for a non-member to register a screenplay is $22.

WRITER'S GUILD OF AMERICA, EAST
555 West 57th Street, Suite 1230
New York, NY 10019-2967
phone: 212-767-7800
website: www.wgaeast.org

WRITER'S GUILD OF AMERICA, WEST
7000 West 3rd Street
Los Angeles, CA 90048-4329
phone: 323-951-4000
website: www.wga.org

After you've worked as hard as you can, then double-checked to make sure it has all the elements audiences want from a block-buster movie, you're ready to move to the next step.

You've got a bullet-proof screenplay that's ready to do battle.

Make Sure Your Screenplay Is Ready

DON'T MAKE BEGINNER MISTAKES

Ambition drives all beginning screenwriters, but you can't rush your screenplay out before it's ready.

Remember, just plain good is never good enough if you want your screenplay to sell.

DAVID BENIOFF *(The 25th Hour)*

One of the mistakes beginning screenwriters make is that they're too formulaic. They end up concentrating on the plot so much, that they end up pushing the characters around.

The other mistake is they have these wonderful, rich characters, but they're making it up as they go along, and they don't really know what the ending is going to be.

For me, my favorite kind of story is when I have a clear sense the writer is taking me on a journey and the writer has a very clear sense of where we're going to end up.

Narrative is a craft, and you have to master it. Part of that is learning what to cut out and learning how to write scenes that propel the reader into the next one.

PHILIP EISNER *(Event Horizon)*

Thinking your script is good before it's really good is a common mistake a lot of beginning screenwriters make. Usually the first tier of readers will be very critical, because they want to be writers or executives. But if they love something, they'll actually champion it, because finding a script for someone is a way to move up.

But the executives who actually make the decisions are reading your script at ten o'clock on a Monday morning. And they're probably reading it in the bathroom because they have to have an opinion for the two o'clock meeting. Your script better be great.

ANDREW MARLOWE *(Air Force One)*

One of the things that beginning screenwriters tend to avoid when they first start writing is enough dramatic conflict. They're uncomfortable having characters really go at each other, so you end up with a story that doesn't have any overarching drama. You end up with a screenplay that's just ... this happened ... then this happened ... then this happened, etc. You find the main character is reactive. They don't have an emotional drive.

Another mistake I've noticed about beginning screenwriters is that many are too impatient and act entitled. Beginning screenwriters should know how the system works in Hollywood. When your script comes into an agency or studio, there's someone who reads it and gives it coverage. Your name will be attached to that and it will go into a data base.

The next time your script comes in, they'll check what you did before to see if it was any good. So if you submit something before it's ready, that people don't like, it's like high school, it goes on your personal record. That means you have to work that much harder on your next script to overcome that bias.

There's also a sense of entitlement. They wonder why nobody bought their screenplay. They have to realize that when they send their script out, there's a guy who's job is on the line. He has to decide how much it will cost to make and if an audience show up if they do.

So you have to build a very compelling case with your screenplay that it's worth taking a gamble on. They have to have some sense they will make a return on their investment. Your screenplay has to read like a movie people will want to see.

SCOTT ROSENBERG *(Con Air)*

Beginning screenwriters always send their scripts out too early. I wrote twelve scripts before I got an agent. I wrote fifteen before I sold one. I wrote seventeen before I had a movie made.

At least once a month, someone will call me and say, "My mother met your mother at a wedding ... yadda yadda ... will you read my screenplay?" And I always ask them how many they've written. It's always their first. Out of respect to my mother, I'll agree to read it. But I also say this: "I promise you, it ain't gonna be good. And I'll never read another one again. You got one shot with me." I read it and it always sucks.

My greatest early success came out of a very personal thing happening to me: my father dying. He died of cancer. *Things to do In Denver When You're Dead* came out of that. After that I wrote *Beautiful Girls*. That came out of the ending of my relationship with my girlfriend of seven years.

I started out trying to imitate Shane Black and Daniel Waters in the beginning, and it was probably a mistake. I wasn't writing what was real to me. In the beginning, I didn't try to get an agent. I had a very Zen like approach. They'll find me when I'm ready.

USE FEEDBACK TO MAKE YOUR SCREENPLAY BETTER

Most screenwriters show their work to a group of trusted readers to get comments and suggestions before sending it out. As we've discussed, it's a way of test-marketing your screenplay with a very small audience to see if it will work with a big audience.

Even the top blockbuster screenwriters know they can make mistakes when they're working all alone writing their screenplay, so most use feedback as a way to catch those mistakes. Feedback is a final safe-guard before hitting the marketplace.

DAVID BENIOFF (The 25th Hour)

I have a best friend who's a novelist, and I give my first draft to him. And this is especially important to young writers. You need to have a reader you can trust. Not a reader who's going to tell you it's great. You need somebody who can tell you the hard and critical truth. You'll always be annoyed, but it's absolutely necessary. Every script I've written has been improved because of feedback.

NEAL BRENNAN (Half Baked)

I give my scripts to four or five friends who are all writers. And what I do is put a questionnaire on the back of the script that asks specific questions so people don't just go, "Yeah, I liked it." And the last question is always this: You're on your death bed; please tell me something about this script you wouldn't ordinarily say.

AKIVA GOLDSMAN *(A Beautiful Mind)*

Everybody needs feedback. Everybody needs mirrors. The selection of who those mirrors are can be a writer's greatest tool. Too friendly a witch behind the glass is as little help as too harsh a witch. If, over the course of your life, you can acquire five good readers, readers you can count on, that's a treasure.

Having good readers is really important so you have a sense of when your screenplay is ready to be released. It's a problem to let it go too early, as it is to hang on too long and keep reworking it.

What I'm looking for is to see if I've gotten what I wanted to lasso. I know what I'm going for in a script, and I can usually tell from the feedback whether I got it or not.

When I wrote *A Beautiful Mind*, it was the most important thing to me personally I'd ever written. So in that case, my readers were really important to me. I was looking at their eyes to see if I had done something extraordinary, because that was my goal for that screenplay.

DAVID HAYTER *(X-Men)*

I don't give my scripts out for feedback. If you give your script to another writer, they will not necessarily give you an objective viewpoint. Another writer will always look at it from the point of view of what they would do. And what they would do is not necessarily what you would do. So I keep my own counsel on whether I think it's working. Then I'll let the studio or the producer be my guide.

DALE LAUNER *(My Cousin Vinny)*

I don't give my screenplays out for feedback, but I do it in a different way. Whenever my friends ask what I'm working on, I'll describe it in a fifteen-to twenty-minute pitch. When I'm doing that, I almost always come up with other ideas. And the person I'm telling the story to will do the same. I find that works a little better than giving someone a script.

ANDREW MARLOWE *(Air Force One)*

I've got a handful of people I've grown to trust. I hand it out to a group of people, some of whom I went to USC with. I have a friend I give it to, and we call him "the barometer." He loves movies. He can't tell you why things don't work, he'll just say, "I started to get bored here." That is incredibly useful to me, because he's my audience. I always ask him where he put the screenplay down. I need to know that, because I need to address those moments so I can hold an audience.

When I get the notes back, I then see which ones are useful. If you get five different sets of notes, that's when it's difficult. But if you get similar notes, then you know there are specific problems you have to address. So then you have to isolate what the problems are and figure out how to fix them.

That's when being a professional and knowing your craft is enormously helpful. Because you're not doing it through intuition. You're doing it through a very specific understanding of craft.

SCOTT ROSENBERG *(Con Air)*

There are five people I give my script to before I send it out: my little brother, whoever the girl I'm seeing is at the time, a couple of other friends and buddies. I put the script aside for about ten days, then I get back their notes. If people agree on something, I'll change it. Hey, if three people tell you you're drunk, lie down.

PART FOUR

WHAT YOU NEED TO KNOW ABOUT HOLLYWOOD

WRITING FOR HOLLYWOOD

"This isn't personal, Kay.
It's business."
—The Godfather

As a blockbuster screenwriter, you have to be as knowledge-able as you can about how the movie business works. In some ways, understanding how Hollywood operates is just as important as your creative abilities, because in the high stakes game of movie-making, you have to know the rules if you want to be a winner.

It's a common saying in Hollywood that screenwriters don't have a lot of power. In many aspects of the business, this is true. Even the most successful top-level screenwriters can't automat-ically get movies made, and they're not the final say during much of the decision-making process.

Screenwriters are part of the much larger team it takes to pro-duce and make a movie. And if a screenwriter's movie happens to become a runaway blockbuster hit, there are always others who will glow much brighter in the surrounding spotlight.

MOVIES ARE COLLABORATIVE

Movies are first and foremost a collaborative effort. The studio, the director, the actors, and all the other creative people are involved, too.

Successful screenwriters understand the team nature of movie-making, and they use it to their advantage. They know they're creating stories for a medium in which one person cannot accomplish everything. The audience has expectations and so does the movie-making system. Talented screenwriters use this knowledge to craft movie stories that appeal to both the audience and the other players in the movie-making process.

One of the key skills that successful screenwriters have to learn is how to work effectively in this highly collaborative environment. It's a talent that's critical when working with other professionals as part of a movie-making team. (The screenwriters will discuss this in more detail at the end of the chapter.)

So while it's true screenwriters don't have all the power, it's not true they don't have any.

THE POWER OF SCREENWRITERS

The main power that screenwriters have is much more personal and private. It's also the most important. It's the power to create the story.

The screenwriter is the person who pulls the creative-trigger that starts it all. They conjure up the imaginary elements that become the story. That's the screenwriter's power. It's the power of being the originator. It's the joy of getting an idea and turning that idea into a big-screen story that entertains and touches millions of people.

The screenwriter also has the power of persuasion. While all the other key players—the studio, the producer, the director, the stars—will all have opinions, the screenwriter knows the story better than anyone else. Successful screenwriters are all passionate champions of their work. As other ideas are voiced during the development stage, screenwriters have to keep the story on track. They do that with their passion and deep understanding of how the story works. All successful screenwriters have learned the importance of having a clear and persuasive voice as their story moves through the various development stages to production. (The screenwriters will reveal in more detail how they have to fight to protect their vision at the end of the chapter.)

THE SCREENWRITER'S GOAL

Being a blockbuster screenwriter is all about one important goal after you've finished writing a screenplay:
Sell it!
No matter how much fun it was to write, you want a producer or studio executive to read your screenplay and love it. And they have to love it, because only then will they buy it. Screenwriting is an art, but it's also an art that needs to be sold to be seen. You're creating a story for an audience. To get to that audience, though, your story first needs to excite the people who will buy it and produce it.

To that end, understanding the marketplace is an on-going goal that's impossible to ignore.

Selling a screenplay is almost always an uphill battle. It's hard if you're a beginner, but even for a seasoned writer it's never a sure thing. For everyone, though, the process is generally the same.

Somebody in the movie industry reads your screenplay and loves it. *Not just likes it, loves it*—because just plain good is never good enough. Then the person who loved it will push it up, the hill to the next person. Then, if that person loves it, they'll push it up too, and so on, until your screenplay finally reaches it's hoped for destination.

The person with the power to buy it.

If you're a beginner, the hill is usually bigger, because you're starting at the bottom. If you're a proven professional, the process is generally shorter.

No matter who you are, though, your screenplay is being judged by people with their own peculiar likes and dislikes. But every movie professional who's reading it is asking the same basic question:

Can this screenplay be a successful movie? That's their job. They're looking for great screenplays. If you write one, they'll be very, very happy. Mainstream movie-making has a large and loosely constructed system for buying and developing screenplays. While the process of selling a screenplay is always different according to how you engage the system, there are several key players you need to be familiar with.

The following chapters will examine the roles various movie industry people play in the screenplay process. More importantly, the chapters will also identify as clearly as possible what the movie industry wants from a blockbuster screenplay.

PITCHING YOUR SCREENPLAY

A skill you'll need to develop to work successfully in the Hollywood system is the ability to "pitch" your movie.

A pitch occurs anytime you verbally describe your screenplay or movie idea to someone who can help you. Pitching is an integral part of the Hollywood movie system, because it's here you have to opportunity to "sell" your screenplay. That's what a pitch is, a verbal sales-talk about your story. All screenwriters pitch, both beginners and those at the very top.

How you pitch depends on the circumstances. Screenwriters with a new movie idea will go in and pitch it to the studios. In this case, they'll describe the key elements and broad structure of the story. If a studio likes it, they'll buy it. The writer will then go write the screenplay. Screenwriters will also go in and pitch for an assignment. Here, too, writers will go into a fair amount of detail about their ideas and overall concept. But pitches are also used when calling a new agent or producer, or even during a chance meeting with someone you want to read your screenplay.

Pitching can be one of your most valuable tools.

For proven screenwriters, it's possible to sell a pitch directly to a producer or a studio. Generally, though, you have to be a screenwriter with a successful track record. If a producer or studio is going to buy a pitch, they usually need some degree of confidence you can deliver.

FROM IDEA TO MILLION DOLLAR $ALE
Scott Rosenberg

As the following example illustrates, in Hollywood, sometimes just telling a great story can be enough to make a million dollar sale.

I sold the highest-selling comedy pitch of all time. It was called *Down and Under*. (Now called *Kangaroo Jack*.) It was about two low-level Mafia guys. I did it with a friend of mine who told me the story. We pitched Nick Cage and Chris Farley. Always use actors instead of just names; they can see it better.

Here's the idea. They had to deliver this packet of money to somebody in the Australian outback. On the way, in a jeep, they end up running over a kangaroo. And these guys are a couple of knuckleheads. One of them is wearing this really wild-looking red blazer. They put the blazer on the dead kangaroo as a goof to take a picture. Except the kangaroo isn't dead. It jumps up and races away. And the money they have to deliver is in an envelope in the red blazer.

I always say about a pitch, if you can let them see the poster, you'll sell it. And that's what our pitch did. You see two crazy guys running after a kangaroo in a blazer.

We went to MGM and they spent the first twenty minutes telling us why they don't buy pitches. When we were finished I called my agent in the parking lot because I was so mad. I thought the meeting had been a big waste of time. But she told me to relax. They bought it for $1.5 million.

The goal in a pitch is always the same: You want to describe your movie story in the most exciting way you can. You want the listener to get pumped-up about what a terrific movie your story would be.

Working in Hollywood

Because the process of making movies is so collaborative, it's not only about the great words that you conjure up and put on the page. Your success will also be influenced by your skills in working with other people.

Blockbuster screenwriters have to navigate their creative vision through an often difficult landscape filled with different points of view. The ability to do this in a way that's both artistically honest and also collaborative is a mega-important part of working at this level of the movie business.

WORKING AS PART OF A TEAM

Not letting ego needlessly get in the way is a key characteristic of successful screenwriters. They know how to be positive and collaborative, and not fight over issues or ideas that are unimportant.

DAVID BENIOFF *(The 25th Hour)*

I think screenwriters would be well advised not to assume the suits are morons. It's interesting, because the publishing world is considered more intellectual, but frankly, I've been more impressed with the people I've met in Hollywood—with exceptions of course. There are a lot of intelligent people working in the movie business. I hear a lot of other screenwriters talk about executives with disdain, and it's wrong. It's also detrimental, because then they start dumbing down their work. Not assuming people are idiots is really important.

You've got to be able to work with other people. Ultimately, a lot of people are needed to make a movie. You need the producers; they're an important part of the puzzle. So if you come into the room with a combative attitude right off the bat—"I'm the writer, I'm the genius ..."—and you treat the other people like they don't know anything, it's not to your benefit. Most of the time you'll find that people have reasonably intelligent things to say. If you don't want to work with other people, you should be writing novels.

AKIVA GOLDSMAN *(A Beautiful Mind)*

Writers fall into two categories. There are writers who like life off the page and those who don't. You're probably going to be better in a meeting if you're in the first group. Mostly, people should think that you're smart and you're good at what you do. You should also try to be a kind person and compassionate, because it's better to be that than not. Then luck will find you.

DAVID HAYTER *(X-Men)*

I find charm, affability, and a clear articulation of your ideas to be invaluable. There are a lot of great writers who get by who are difficult and cantankerous. But I find the process to be far more enjoyable, and the final movie to be far more satisfying, if you were able to enjoy it all the way through, and your partners were able to enjoy it, too.

You can spend the whole time fighting with the studio and their ideas, and creating a malicious atmosphere with them. That's fine for artistic integrity. But will that make it easier for your artistic ideas to get across? Absolutely not.

A studio is like a person. If their egos get bruised and they get angry and find you difficult, you will find it very difficult to make the movie you want to make. So I find creative freedom much more when the studio feels I have their money in mind and protected in my own creative vision. They give me artistic freedom because they know we're both on the same side.

JIM KOUF (Rush Hour)

You have to be able to work with people. The screenwriters who have the longest careers are the ones who don't burn bridges along the way. You have to fight for what you believe in, but it's not personal, and you have to know when to walk away. People work with people they like. When I was first starting out, I probably made a mistake with some of the battles I picked.

ANDREW MARLOWE (Air Force One)

A lot of the time it's essential that you have some P.T. Barnum in your personality. That is, you know how to sell. I think it's hard if you're not good in a room. People are looking not just at how good the material is, but also if they want to spend a year of their life with you trying to get the movie made.

I'm not a social guy. I'm not a good glad-hander and small-talker. But I found that I needed to acquire those skills in order to get to the levels and have the access that I want to have. To be able to meet someone you've never met before in a pitch session and put them at ease helps enormously. I've found I have to cultivate those skills to be in a position to do the things I want to do.

In the development process, serving several different political agendas at once is very difficult. Having a strong producer, a strong studio executive, a strong director and star, and having them all pulling you in different directions, can be a reality of the business.

And you have to negotiate all these different agendas into a clear and clean dramatic through-line. The process is filled with tremendous egos that are easily bruised.

And those egos are mine-fields that you have to politically negotiate through. It has nothing to do with good writing. It has nothing to do with good storytelling. But it has everything to do with getting the movie made.

ED SOLOMON *(Men In Black)*

In any kind of job, your success rate is higher if you have certain personal skills. I try to be open-hearted. I try to be grateful for the chance to work with other people. I try to be appreciative. I try to be understanding of other people's situation. I try to be respectful.

YOU ALSO HAVE TO KNOW WHEN TO FIGHT

But being a good collaborator doesn't mean you give up every time someone has a different point of view. In the crowded process of movie-making, the screenwriter has to maintain a strong creative vision to keep the story on track. Blockbuster screenwriters don't fight needlessly and recklessly, but when they do fight, they fight to win.

PHILIP EISNER *(Event Horizon)*

I've gotten a lot more combative as I've gotten older. I've stopped assuming that someone knows better than me, at least with my own material. I know the material better than anyone else.

AKIVA GOLDSMAN (A Beautiful Mind)

I can be pretty stubborn. But I also know when to give up. It depends on what I'm fighting for and who I'm fighting. But I get to fight because of where I am now. It's different if you're just starting out. If that's the case, you should state what you believe as clearly and as articulately as possible and then do the other thing if they're not buckling.

DAVID GOYER (Blade)

I fight like a rabid animal now. And I've walked away from movies if I violently disagree with something. That's something that, if you make a certain amount of money, is a luxury you can afford. There are projects I have my name on that I wished I'd taken my name off. But in the beginning, you think you need credits, so you don't. There are projects that I'm embarrassed by because they got ruined by the actors, or the director, or something else.

Nowadays, I won't hesitate to take my name off something if I don't believe in it. I don't recommend it all the time.

It's interesting. If you're willing to walk away and show you believe that strongly about something, it will cause people on the other side of the table to question their beliefs. I actually walked off *Blade* for a week.

DAVID HAYTER (X-Men)

If I feel that something is intrinsic to the success of the story and they want to change it, I will fight to the death. I try to keep it from getting personal. I just try to illustrate that the reason I'm passionate about it is because it's integral to the story.

Otherwise, if it's something else, I'll do it. If I can change something that will make them happy and it doesn't cost me anything story-wise, I'll do it. I'll change everything I can to save up battle-strength for the things that are vitally important.

SCOTT ROSENBERG (Con Air)

I fight very hard. I've quit a lot of movies. But you have to know when to pick and choose. If you're telling a story about my family, the Rosenbergs, coming over from the old country, don't fuck with that. But if you're paying me a million bucks to rewrite *Spiderman*, then fine, fuck with me. You have to be emotionally invested to do good work, but at the same time you have to emotionally divest yourself when it's work for hire. You have to understand your role.

ED SOLOMON (Men in Black)

Unfortunately for the screenwriter, your only option is to try to argue your point. You don't have the trump card. The director has the trump card. You fight as hard as you can, but if you're too much of a pain in the ass, they'll just get rid of you.

LEARN HOW TO PITCH YOUR MOVIE IDEA

Knowing how to pitch is an essential tool for any screenwriter working in the Hollywood system. It's the shorthand way of selling your movie idea to another player in the process. Just like in your screenplay, the goal of pitching is to tell your movie story in the most exciting way possible. It should communicate what's special and entertaining about your story.

You don't have to be an actor, but you do have to show that you've created a story you love and millions other people will love, too.

DAVID BENIOFF *(The 25th Hour)*

You just want to know the story as well as possible. You want to just go in there and tell the story in the most dramatic way possible. It's got to be something you're passionate about and you want to communicate that passion.

I'm not a great orator and I don't think it really matters. It's tough to go into a room if the people in the room haven't read anything you've written, because then it's all purely hypothetical. But if they've read something you've written and liked it, that's the best. Then when you pitch, if they like the idea, they already know you can deliver.

That's what happened when I sold a pitch about the Trojan War. (Now called *Troy*.) I certainly wasn't very eloquent. In fact, the executive was yawning during my pitch. I thought he was going to call security and throw me out on my ass. But he'd read my stuff and liked it. He liked the idea, too, and bought it.

AKIVA GOLDSMAN *(A Beautiful Mind)*

I can respond to pitching from both sides, because I also get a lot of pitches as a producer.

The act of pitching is the same as the act of writing. You have to tell somebody the story. You have to involve them in the story. And you should be able to do it in about twenty minutes. I try to be pretty specific for the first few scenes and then move into broad strokes. I also believe you should know your story in far more detail than you pitch, so if they ask you a question, you can confidently answer it.

DAVID HAYTER *(X-Men)*

Before I'm ready to pitch a new story to somebody, I want to know who the main character is, what's his problem, what's the course of the story, what's the ending in very basic, broad strokes. And I want a cool world, a place to set it in. Once I have that, I'll go in and pitch it to a studio. If they like it, they'll hire me to write it.

ANDREW MARLOWE *(Air Force One)*

Beginners tend to over prepare and use a lot of detail. What I've discovered is that pitching is less telling the story and more selling the story.

Your job in a pitch is to get the guy sitting across from you to open his wallet and give you a bunch of money. To do that you have to give him the moments that he can sell to his boss as moments they can put in the trailer to sell the movie. It's all about getting an audience.

When I was working on *Air Force One* the producer was taking his kids to the same school that Arnold Schwarzenegger's kids go to. They had become friendly.

The producer came to me and said, "I want to do a movie with Arnold Schwarzenegger."

With Arnold, he generally plays the same iconic character. He has stuff he's really good at and you want to play to those strengths. Especially if you're going to invest $100 million, because you want to get some money back. So I started thinking about who would be a good new bad guy for him to fight. And then I thought, well, the ultimate bad guy is the Devil. Wouldn't it be fun to see Arnold go up against the Devil?

Here's the pitch. I said, imagine you're in the theater and the lights go down. You see the previews for coming attractions. The music swells. You see glory shots of New York City. The Empire State Building. Central Park. Park Avenue. Then the narrator says, "It's New Year's Eve in New York City . . . and it's about to get a little hotter!" BOOM! An entire city block goes up in flames . . . letters start flying at us . . . Showdown . . . Schwarzenegger and Satan . . . and there's Arnold . . . surrounded by flames looking down the barrel of a very big gun . . . *"I'm sending you back to Hell!"*

They bought it.

TACTICS AND STRATEGIES

"Question: What is the primary goal?
Answer: To win the game."
—Wargames

I'm sure most blockbuster screenwriters will confess a little bit of luck helped them at some point along the way in their careers. They were in the right place at the right time and an unexpected quirk of fate bumped their career in a helpful way.

They'll also agree that you have to have talent. It's the essential quality that gets you noticed and will sustain your career. But talent alone is never enough, and this is advice that blockbuster screenwriters will all shout at the top of their lungs:

You have to work hard.
You have to be determined.
You have to be tenacious.

Because these are the other qualities that every top-level screenwriter shares. You can't control luck, but you can control how much of yourself you're willing to give to achieve your goal. The truth is, it has to be an all or nothing decision. As we've said all along, there's nothing meek or modest about a blockbuster movie. That also applies to the effort required to start your career.

You have to be the hero in your own life-changing story. You're trying to do something that a lot of people also want to do. Screenplays are pouring into the Hollywood system every day, written by people just like you. Some of them will make it, but the staggering majority won't. Like most things in life, it's a competition, and only the most determined and hardest working will win.

Anyone who's spent any amount of time in the movie-making world knows it's not a place for wishy-washy, timid personalities. The size and complexity of the process is enormous. As such, the people who become successful have to be strong willed and fiercely determined.

To get a movie made, a producer usually has to work for years bringing the story to the screen. It's always a complicated task that's riddled with constant failures and setbacks, but the successful producers never give up, which is why they're successful.

As a screenwriter, you have to do the same thing.

Never give up.

YOU HAVE TO PRODUCE YOUR CAREER

For many beginning screenwriters, this comes as a bit of a shock. Most writers, by nature, are cerebral and low-key. They enjoy the mental and imaginative challenges of creating and writing stories, but it usually stops there. They'd prefer that all the arguments, battles, and confrontations in their life exist only on the page.

As a blockbuster screenwriter, though, you have to be a fighter. Up until now that fight has been mostly in your head. You've worked your hardest and written the best screenplay you can.

Now you have to fight to get people to read it.

Just like being a movie producer, there are no hard and fast rules to follow, because every movie has a different path to the movie screen. It's the same for the beginning screenwriter producing and creating a career.

Following are beginning tactics and strategies for how to fight the good fight that every screenwriter starting out has to face.

It's part of the process of becoming a screenwriter.. No matter what a successful screenwriter appears like on the outside, scratch below the surface and you'll find a fiercely competitive personality whose ambition and tenacity got them to where they are. So if you want to join the club, you have to put on your gloves and fight for what you want.

David Hayter's blockbuster career had a very unusual beginning. Unlike most screenwriters, he didn't use a spec screenplay to get his first break in the business. While his story is a big exception to the way it's normally done, it does show how a beginning screenwriter can use his determination and talent to get in the door. There's no one way to start a screenwriting career. This is how David Hayter did it.

I started out as an actor. That's all I ever wanted to be. But it was tough. I wasn't getting the work I wanted.

In 1997 I produced and starred in a movie to try to help my career. The script for the movie was a script that Bryan Singer had been interested in as a student filmmaker, and he ended up coming on as an executive producer of our movie. It did well on the film festival circuit, but it was never bought for distribution.

So, at the time, I was really poor and desperate, because I had been out of acting for two years and had nothing going. It was bad. I called Bryan, who was now working on *X-Men*, and I asked him for a job. I said I'd do anything, answer the phones, drive a truck, I didn't care. I just really needed the money. He said sure. So I came in and started answering the phones.

After I'd been there for a couple of weeks, I mentioned to Bryan that I was a big fan of the *X-Men* comics and if he ever wanted to talk about anything, I'd be honored.

Because of that, he ended up using me as his driver instead. He said his assistant wasn't interested in how movies were put together and he knew I was. So I started driving him around to all the different special effect houses he was working with.

While we were doing this, Bryan kept talking about the script, trying to work through whatever problems he was having. One day, I made a couple of suggestions about a new scene that I thought might help. I just threw it out as conversation. Bryan thought for a second, then said, "Good. Go write it." I thought he was joking, of course, so I didn't.

The next day, he called me at the office and said, "Did you write that scene for me?" I told him I didn't think he was really serious. "No, I need it. Go write it. Get it done." So I spent all that day writing this three-page scene that I carefully crafted and perfected. I sent it to him and he put it in the screenplay.

Over the next couple of months, I started going to the story meetings under the guise of just taking notes for him. Then, unbeknownst to the studio, I would go home and write until two o'clock in the morning. I was doing all the rewrites on the script.

After about three months, the producer, Ralph Winter, calls me in the office and says, "Can you give me a script with everything you've done highlighted." I gave it to him the next day. At this point, it was half the script. And this is in no way a bad reflection on Christopher MacQuarrie, the original writer, because he's brilliant. It's just that Bryan Singer, as a director, continues to develop and work on the screenplay right up until the premier. So the producer went to the studio and said they had to make a deal with me or I could sue.

At the time, I was still working as an assistant making $525 a week. The studio brings me in. They're not thrilled this is going on, because they don't know who I am. They tell me they're going to give me $35,000 which is the minimum Writer's Guild rewrite fee. They said to not ask for a penny more. I remember walking out thinking, oh my god, $35,000! I was thrilled to get that deal.

I flew up to Canada. I was on set for eight months tweaking the script. It was an unbelievable feeling. I was on the set coming up with new lines for the actors. During this whole time, everyone is telling me that I will never ever get credit for the script.

In the end, with the help and support of Chris MacQuarrie and Ed Solomon, the two writers before me, I did. Here's what's amazing. Both Chris and Ed, in their letters to the Guild arbitration committee, said that I was the architect of the movie and I deserved credit. And they did this with significant cost to themselves in terms of credit bonuses and other things. It was one of the most noble things I've ever seen in my life.

After that, I got a call from an executive at the studio. He said, "Do you know what you're going to be making as residuals on this movie?" It ended being a little less than a million dollars.

At the time I had nothing. That much money was unfathomable. I couldn't even fit it into my brain.

At this point though, the industry was unsure about me. They wondered if I had just written on the backs of Bryan Singer, Chris MacQuarrie, and Ed Solomon. The question on everybody's mind was whether I could do it without them. What changed that was the *Hulk* script. I was brought in to write that and Ang Lee signed on to direct it. He's a great director. He directed *Sense and Sensibility* and *Crouching Tiger, Hidden Dragon*. After that I was an A-list screenwriter.

My next big deal is for the *Watchmen*. (*Watchmen* is a comic-book adaptation that's been dragged through Hollywood development hell for the last fifteen years.) It's a $1.3-million-dollar deal, with me writing and directing.

THE SELF-STARTER STRATEGY

Rather than waiting for opportunity to knock on the door, which almost never, ever happens, it's always better to just go ahead and open the door yourself.

Hollywood has a long history of legendary ways people have scaled the walls to get inside. Or if they couldn't find a way over the wall, they snuck through a backdoor they created themselves. For the screenwriter, the task of "breaking in" can seem overwhelming and intimidating.

Just remember, you have what they want.

What everybody is looking for is a great screenplay that can become a great movie. So don't be misguided or shy about your worth or importance. If you have talent, that's what Hollywood needs to survive. Even if you're a complete unknown, have confidence and pride in what you have to offer.

Believe in your yourself and your screenplay.

Some screenwriters have self-started their careers by believing in themselves when the system wouldn't. Rather than depending on others, they just went ahead and produced a movie from their screenplay themselves.

A good example is *The Blair Witch Project*, co-written and directed by Eduardo Sanchez and Daniel Myrick. While the movie's amazing box-office success is part of blockbuster history, the movie-makers started out at the back of the pack. They were college students in the film program at the University of Central Florida. The movie was shot for $35,000 in eight days, using friends and college equipment.

But the two unknowns didn't just stop at making the movie themselves, they also figured out a way to make it successful. They used the festival circuit and the Internet to build a pre-release buzz that made the mock-documentary a horror movie hit that's grossed $140 million—making it more successful than big studio movies like *Godzilla* and *Close Encounters of the Third Kind*.

Another example of beginner determination is Robert Rodriguez, who also started out far away from Hollywood, in this case as a film student at the University of Texas. To raise money to shoot his first movie, he checked himself into a medical research center, where he was paid to be a human guinea pig to test new pharmaceutical drugs. With the help of friends he was able to raise $7,000, and this was the budget of *El Mariachi*, which he wrote, produced, directed, shot, and edited. Despite the tiny budget, the movie generated the attention that started his career. From this small-scale beginning, he's gone on to much bigger things, like writing and directing the third *Spy Kids* movie with a $40-million budget.

What the previous examples show most of all is the importance of believing in yourself at the beginning of your career. The filmmakers were all talented, but it wasn't just talent that got their careers going. It was confidence and a fierce determination to be what they wanted to be. So rather than waiting for someone to grant them the opportunity, they did it themselves. They spent their own money, also produced and directed, all because they wanted to see what they'd written be what they dreamed it would be.

A movie.

CONTESTS, FELLOWSHIPS, FESTIVALS, EVENTS

Another tactic is to take advantage of the screenwriting contests, fellowships, competitions, seminars, and events that are available. They're out there, ready and waiting. If you don't know about them already, you need to.

As a beginning screenwriter, you want to get your screenplay and yourself to as many places as possible where contacts and opportunities can occur.

In the beginning of your career, cast as wide a net as possible, learning as you go, and meeting people who are in the world you want to be a part of.

Like any business, you want to build your resume and interact with people that can help you. Screenwriting contests are one of the ways you can do that. Like everything else in the screenwriting world, the number of contests has increased dramatically, and more seem to pop up all the time.

Not all of them, however, are worth the expense of the entry fee. Make sure you do some research about any contest you're thinking about entering. Your best bet is usually to stay with the top few that are the most reputable.

Contests have been a career starter for a number of successful screenwriters in recent years.

The top contests and competitions are monitored by various agencies and studios, so it's a way to get exposure. More importantly, it's a way to sell your screenplay from that exposure. Having recognition from one of the recognized screenwriting competitions is a definite advantage when marketing yourself and your work.

Following are the contests, competitions and fellowships that are considered the best.

NICHOLL FELLOWSHIPS
Academy of Motion Picture Arts and Sciences
8949 Wilshire Boulevard
Beverly Hills, CA 90211-1972
Phone: 310-247-3000

This is the pre-eminent screenwriting competition, sponsored by the same organization as the Academy Awards. Past winners include Andrew Marlowe, who's interviewed in this book, and Mike Rich, the screenwriter of *Finding Forrester* and *The Rookie*.

AUSTIN HEART OF FILM SCREENPLAY COMPETITION
1604 Nueces
Austin, Texas 78701
phone: 512-478-4795

The competition is part of a weekend screenwriting festival in October, in which top screenwriters participate in a wide variety of panel discussions, pitch sessions, and informal meetings targeted to aspiring screenwriters. Highly recommended.

CHESTERFIELD WRITERS FILM PROJECT
Chesterfield Film Co.
1158 26th Street, Box 544
Santa Monica, CA 90403
Phone: 213-683-3977

Sponsored by Paramount Pictures, this competition also includes a year-long writing workshop. Well regarded and sought after.

PROJECT GREENLIGHT
LivePlanet, Inc.
7610 Beverly Boulevard
P.O. Box 48649
Los Angeles, CA 90048
Website: www.projectgreenlight.com

Run in conjunction with the **HBO** show *Project Greenlight*. The winning screenwriter is filmed documentary style shooting the movie of their script. So if your script wins, exposure (every week on HBO) is guaranteed.

SUNDANCE INSTITUTE
Film Feature Institute
8857 West Olympic Boulevard
Beverly Hills, CA 90211
Phone: 310-360-1969

This is a very prestigious program that's geared to more personal and writer-driven projects. Created by Robert Redford to support the independent filmmaker.

The above are the most reputable and closely monitored by the movie industry. They've become another valid and accepted way for beginning screenwriters to get their script out into the marketplace for evaluation and exposure.

There are dozens of other contests and competitions, but these should be approached with more scrutiny. Judge the credentials and details of the contest before entering.

MOVIEBYTES.COM
Is a good source for a complete listing of screenwriting contests and competitions.

Along with contests and competitions, it's also worthwhile to attend any kind of screenwriting, or film, festival and event. With the always growing popularity of screenwriting and movies, there's also been a growing number of screenwriting seminars, film festivals, and other kinds of events.

Whether it's attending a weekend seminar with Robert McKee, a well-known screenwriting teacher; going to a local film festival; or taking a screenwriting course at the local college, there are many ways to meet people and make contacts.

If you want to be part of the movie world, start going anywhere and everywhere that connects you with other screenwriters, teachers, actors, agents, directors, producers, and anybody else that might be helpful.

And don't be shy about who you are and what you want to be. Let people know about your screenwriting goals and dreams. Talk about what you've written with passion and excitement. Get the word out to anybody that will listen. Because you never know when someone will be able to help you. Or they may have a cousin, or friend in the business they can introduce you to.

CREATIVE SCREENWRITING, SCR(I)PT, FADE-IN
The screenwriting magazines are a good place to find out about seminars and screenwriting events.

WWW.FILMFESTIVALS.COM
This site offers a comprehensive listing of film festivals.

What you're doing with the above tactics and strategies is adding to your credentials as a screenwriter and developing contacts.

This is as much a part of the process of being a screenwriter as writing the screenplay—at least in the beginning. It's your responsibility to get your script and yourself out to anyplace that can be beneficial.

Exposure is what you're going for, both for yourself and your work. In the beginning, this is almost always a frustrating and haphazard exercise filled with rejection and closed doors.

That's why the screenwriters who eventually succeed are the ones who work the hardest and persevere.

MOVING TO LOS ANGELES

For most screenwriters, the decision about whether to move to Los Angeles is one of the bigger issues they will face at the beginning of their careers.

It's not an easy decision to make, because there's no clear-cut answer. There are specific benefits and drawbacks involved, and each will have varying degrees of importance, based on the individual.

On the most basic level, it's a life-changing decision, so it shouldn't be made without serious thought and preparation. But it's also a decision that puts you at the epicenter of the movie industry, so it shouldn't be dismissed without an understanding of what's involved.

Why You Should Immediately Move to Los Angeles

IT'S WHERE THE ACTION IS Los Angeles is the movie-making capital of the world, so if you want to write movies, it makes sense to be there. Potential contacts and opportunities are everywhere. Being there also sends a clear message to anyone you meet. You've committed your life and your lifestyle to being a screenwriter. You've put your money (or lack of it), where your heart is.

You can get a job at a studio or any other kind of movie-related company. It can be as a temp worker or anything else that gets you on the inside. Many beginning screenwriters have used these kinds of entry-level jobs to make contacts and get their material read.

AGENTS PREFER IT Agents definitely prefer that their clients live in the Los Angeles area, especially those who are in the early stage of building their careers. The reason is simple logistics. As a beginning screenwriter, one of the agent's objectives is to introduce you to the various people in the industry who can give you work. And the on-going process of meeting with producers, studio executives, and others is simply easier when you can jump in a car instead of an airplane.

Why You Should Stay Right Where You Are

LOS ANGELES IS WHERE THE ACTION IS *Except you're not part of it.* The old cliché about Los Angeles is that everybody has a screenplay they want to sell. For the beginning screenwriter, rushing out to Los Angeles before you're ready may be more emotionally wearying than helpful.

The sheer competitiveness of the environment can be frustrating and draining. There's nothing fun or spiritually rewarding about being on the outside looking in. It may be better to stay put and only move when you have a specific reason to. Or at least write in the more supportive surroundings of where you live until you have a great blockbuster screenplay, or two, or three to take with you.

Just like writing a screenplay, getting your screenplay sold and breaking into the business is a process. In the beginning, you want to consider all the different ways you can focus your life on making it happen.

Your first big break can come lots of different ways, so your efforts should be energetic and broad. Believe in yourself as a screenwriter and do everything you can to make that belief

known to anybody that can help. That's where you start.
Selling yourself is part of selling your screenplay.

Moving To Los Angeles

You can begin your screenwriting career anywhere, but moving to Los Angeles will probably help. Los Angeles is where the business you want to be a part of has made it's home, so maybe it should be your home, too.

It's a personal decision and never an easy one for a beginning screenwriter to make. But if you truly want to write big movies, then you might have to make a big decision about where to live.

DAVID BENIOFF *(The 25th Hour)*

Being from New York, I actually bought into the belief that the people in Los Angeles are all retarded. Actually, a lot of the LA stereotypes are true, but they don't apply to everyone. It's important that screenwriters be open-minded about it and not come here thinking they're only going to be dealing with mental idiots.

AKIVA GOLDSMAN *(A Beautiful Mind)*

In the beginning, living in Los Angeles is vital. I went out there for two weeks and ended up staying for ten years. That's where the business is. You're in the mix. Until you make your name, part of who you are is "who you are." People have to read your stuff and meet you. They have to think, he seems like a nice guy to work with, he seems smart.

DAVID GOYER *(Blade)*

Networking is important. I tend to be a little bit of an introvert, so I've really had to force myself to get out there and shake hands. Hollywood is definitely an industry that's built on relationships. It's important to know who you're selling to.

JIM KOUF *(Rush Hour)*

If you want to be a screenwriter, move to Los Angeles. That's the most important advice I can give to any screenwriter. Come out here and do everything you can to get a job in the industry. Be a production assistant, do anything. But move here to get some kind of job in the movies.

First of all, it will teach you first hand what the process is all about. As a writer, it's really helpful to understand all the different components involved in making a movie. It helps to understand what things cost, what's actually done on a set. It makes you a better screenwriter.

Look, I get letters all the time from people out in the country asking me to read their script. But I just can't do it. I don't have the time, because I'm busy writing my own stuff. But if somebody I know asks me to read their script, then I probably will. If you're sending your screenplay from somewhere out in the country, they're just going to end up in a pile.

If you want to be a screenwriter, move to Los Angeles. It's that simple.

ANDREW MARLOWE *(Air Force one)*

I think living in Los Angeles is important. It's important to be a part of the community, because you end up becoming acquaintances and friends with people who will give you work and who you can bring projects to. It's much easier to call up one of your good friends and say, "Hey, I've got this great idea. Are you interested?"

And when you're first starting out, it's essential to be there, because you have to be available for meetings. When somebody calls for a meeting and you have to fly in, or you have to ask the studio to pay for you to fly in, you're handicapped. It's the guy down the street who's going to be there on call who will get the job. Because if every time they want to talk to you, or give you notes, they have to fly you in, it's a pain.

AGENTS NEED YOU AS MUCH AS YOU NEED THEM

*"What we have here is a
failure to communicate"*
—Cool Hand Luke

As a beginning screenwriter, getting an agent is usually the single most frustrating and challenging part of starting your career.

At this point though, we need to first focus on the role agents play in the movie-making process. Like all the chapters in this section, the objective is to be educated about the how the system works, so you can be a smarter and more effective screenwriter.

WHAT AGENTS DO

Agents represent their clients, in this case screenwriters, in the business of selling their work and talents to the movie industry. While it's possible to sell a screenplay without an agent, having one, the right one, is a definite advantage.

An agent has two basic jobs.

The first is to sell the writer's work to the industry and find ongoing work that will build the writer's career. If a screenwriter has a hot new blockbuster spec script, it's the agent's job to build a buzz and get it bought for the highest price. This involves knowing who the key players are, who will respond most strongly to the material, and developing the best strategy for who to send the script to. The agent also actively looks for new work in the form of original assignments and rewrite jobs. The agent sets up meetings for the writer to pitch new ideas or discuss potential assignments.

Secondly, it's the agent's job to negotiate any business deal involving the writer's services. This will include negotiating payment, the completion schedule, and various other specifics.

In broad terms, the agent's job is to be an expert on the marketplace. They keep track of the ongoing ebb and flow of who's where, who's buying what, what's selling for how much, etc. They do this by actively being a part of the moviemaking community. An agent builds expertise and effectiveness through personal and business relationships, networking at functions and social events, and staying up-to-date on all aspects of the movie business.

For the beginning screenwriter, getting an agent can be a daunting task, for lots of different reasons. Many screenwriters get their first break without one. As you're developing your career, include getting an agent as one of your goals, but also don't let it be the only goal to the exclusion of everything else.

WHAT AGENTS WANT

To make money. That's it.

And it's not a bad thing, because they do it by fighting as hard as they can for the writers they represent. When the writer succeeds, the agent succeeds. If an agent's writers aren't working and making money, then the agent is feeling the pressure just as much as the writers.

But this is also one of the reasons it's so difficult for new screenwriters to find representation.

For the agent, taking on a new screenwriter comes with mostly challenges and unknowns. The new writer may have written a great spec script, but there's also the possibility it's the only great story they have to tell.

There are a countless questions the agent has to think about. Will the new screenwriter work hard? Will they work well with others? Are they dependable? Are they worth all the time and work it will take to launch their careers?

Introducing a new screenwriter to the industry takes time and patience. It means setting up meet-and-greet meetings, and sending out the writer's work.

Agents know from experience that all this effort on behalf of a new screenwriter is a toss of the dice. It might pay off, or it might end up being a total waste of time that could have been much better spent working for their proven writers.

So what's a new screenwriter to do?

Try to get an agent.

The roadblocks are there, but that's all they are, just challenges that can be overcome. It happens all the time. New screenwriters can and do find representation.

That's because the audience is always looking for new and exciting movie stories, so Hollywood has to constantly be on the lookout for new voices and talent. Agents especially. Agents know that producers and studios get excited at the appearance of a new screenwriter with a great new blockbuster screenplay.

When this happens, it reflects well on the agent as well as the writer, because he or she has proven an ability to discover new talent, which is a vital Hollywood skill.

Also remember this when you're selling your talents and screenplay to agents: Agents are selling every day, too, so underneath it all, most understand the process and respect what it takes. In Hollywood, everybody has to sell something, or movies wouldn't get made.

So sell your part of the movie-making process with all the effort and confidence it takes.

HOW AGENTS JUDGE NEW CLIENTS

When considering a new screenwriter, most agents evaluate the submitted work in two broad ways.

The first is on all the basic fundamentals. This is the craft of writing a professional screenplay. In the ultra-competitive business of movies, there's no room for sloppy beginners. Your screenplay has to be professional in every way. This means correct format, grammar, spelling, etc. These are details that can't be ignored.

They're an instant turnoff to any professional reading your work. You're a writer, and nothing reflects poorly on your talents quicker than weak language skills.

Then agents judge the fundamentals of the story itself. Are the characters and dialogue compelling and entertaining? Is the descriptive writing clear and vivid? Does the story have narrative power? Does it connect with a broad audience? Is the story big enough to be a movie?

The second way agents evaluate scripts is based on a single word. *Talent.* Talent is that special ability that gifted writers have. It's the ability to create a story that's surprising and deeply engaging. One quality that always impresses an agent is the ability to create a great story, in a fresh and different way.

As we discussed in chapter 12, it's called "the writer's voice." The search in blockbuster movie-making is always for great new stories that are told in an exciting new "voice."

In the following interview, one of the most successful agents in Hollywood covers all the aspects of selling million dollar blockbuster screenplays. He identifies specifically what agents look for in a screenplay and what qualities you need to have to be a successful screenwriter.

Emile Gladstone, with The Broder-Webb-Chervin-Silberman Agency in Beverly Hills, is one of the premier film literary agents in the country and a recognized expert on blockbuster screenwriting. Representing a select group of A-list writers, he's responsible for well over forty spec screenplay and pitch sales, including some of the industry's biggest million dollar sales in the last five years. Some notable client movies are *The Game*, *There's Something About Mary*, *I Spy*, and *Terminator 3*.

There are many different qualities you look for in a script. Every script is a different animal, so it's hard to generalize. There are extremely small, redemptive stories that have sold for a lot of money, so I don't want to steer people away from a story they want to write.

But if you're looking at something from just a commercial or marketing standpoint, then you're looking for a movie story that knows what it is and goes after a certain audience. The story has a visceral impact. It makes you laugh or cry. It scares the shit out of you or it thrills you.

Beginning screenwriters make the mistake of thinking that a story that's interesting to them will be interesting to a mass audience. Because their professor in college praised their small story that was so precious to them, they think everyone else will like it, too. They won't. The bottom line is you're not skilled enough to give that small story justice.

It all starts with a great idea. That's the hardest part. I will tell you point-blank that writing is easy. Coming up with a great idea and creating the story is hard.

Your main character is extremely important. They have to be castable. It has to be somebody that has a relatability to the audience. It's human relatability.

It's one of the chief words we use at the agency in the development process. We make sure the reader relates to the screenplay as the viewer would relate to the movie. And whatever journey the hero is on, whether it's being chased by Jason, or having to save the girl, or trying to get laid, it's a challenge the audience can relate to.

The writer's personality is also important. I've sent so many writers to acting class. As the writer on a movie, you have to be big in a room. You have to have a presence in the room. You can't just go in and stare at your shoes and be quiet.

Once you sell a screenplay, that's just the beginning of your career. The bread and butter of a screenwriter in Hollywood is writing on assignment. It involves rewriting other specs, writing adaptations of magazine articles and books, writing sequels, prequels, and remakes. The majority of the money my clients make is on assignments.

You don't get an assignment just by being talented. You get an assignment by being talented and narrowing in on what's going to make the room excited and pounding it home. Also remember that, the executives will have to work with you for the next nine to eighteen months, so they'd better like you. They better want to hang out with you.

When you sell a million dollar screenplay, you generally need more than one buyer. The last couple of scripts I sold for a lot of money were not in bidding wars. They involved someone making a pre-emptive bid, knowing that other people in the industry wanted to buy it as well.

Usually, million dollar screenplays are not only conceptual, they're also good. The writer isn't just writing for themselves. They're writing for the marketplace. They're writing for the audience.

Genre is also important. It's the number one word. Genre is exactly what you look for. Comedies that make you laugh. Action stories that get you excited. Don't do a horror-musical-western-comedy. That's a big rookie error, too. Stick to the genre. Be a student of genre movies. Make sure there's a trailer in your movie. Talking heads may be fun for a writer, but they're awful for a viewer.

It's often very arbitrary how a spec screenplay is sold. If a new studio president gets their job and wants to flex their muscles, they might buy a script for a lot of money to make a splash in the marketplace.

There are a lot of nuances that exist that have nothing to do with the actual material itself. It's not just about a good piece of writing. It's about a marketing friendly piece of material that a studio can plug into its marketing distribution machine.

For that reason, you can write a mediocre script and have it bought for a million dollars. Because it's not about excellent writing, it's about a marketable concept.

An A-list screenwriter will get anywhere from $600,000 to a $1.4 million for an original screenplay, adaptation of a book, or a remake of a movie. There are plenty of writers who get $100,000 or more a week just to be on set. They work with the director and actors, punching up dialogue.

Living in Los Angeles is very important if you want to make a living as a screenwriter in the Hollywood system. There are plenty of people who live and work in New York, and they do very well, but they make choices. It's quality of life versus getting that extra job. A lot of meetings are set at the last second, and you have to be there.

I believe that a screenwriter has to live in Los Angeles in the beginning of their career.

I've never signed a client from a query letter. We throw them away. You have no idea how many we get.

Buy the *Hollywood Creative Directory*. It lists all the producers and all their staff. Be a student of the marketplace.

If you're writing a big concept comedy, you know that Brian Grazer is a really good producer for those. Look for who is the lowest member of the team, who's at the bottom of the list, because that's the person most likely to read your screenplay.

If they like it, those are the guys who are going to send it to me. I get my clients from producers, lawyers, and other writers. You might get lucky with a query letter, but don't rely on it as your only means of getting an agent.

AGENTS HELP THOSE WHO HELP THEMSELVES

Agents are key players in Hollywood so it's a necessary pursuit for all aspiring screenwriters. Having an agent sends a clear message to any movie professional that you're a professional, too.

But getting an agent is not a magical guarantee that your career will then skyrocket to the blockbuster stratosphere. You have to work hard, and so does your agent. It's a mistake to believe that getting an agent will magically jump-start your career. Agents are just one step up the ladder to screenwriting success. It's your job to write great screenplays, because only then will the agent have what it takes to make you successful.

CHOOSING THE RIGHT AGENCY

While most beginning screenwriters will be happy and gratified to sign with any agent willing to represent their work, there are some broad classifications that are worth noting and considering.

First of all, make sure that any agent you approach is legitimate. Agencies are required by law to be bonded and licensed with the state. This forbids them from taking any kind of registration fee from a client. You also want to only deal with agencies that are a signatory of the Writer's Guild of America, Inc., agreement. This will also protect you from dealing with agencies that don't conform to industry standards.

Like any activity where there's a demand for services, you have to be vigilant and careful about who you form a partnership with.

Secondly, agencies fall into two broad categories.

Smaller agencies, which only handle writers, are called literary or boutique agencies in California. In New York the small agencies that handle screenwriters are called theatrical agencies.

Larger agencies, such as CAA and William Morris, handle writers, too, but also represent directors, actors, and producers.

The benefit of being at a small literary agency is that you and your screenplay are the primary focus. Because the agents work exclusively with writers, they tend to be more understanding and supportive of the screenwriter's part in the process. They'll usually fight harder for you and your work, because that's their only allegiance.

The downside is less overall clout and power. The smaller agencies, by definition, don't have the size and power to package movies as quickly or as easily as the larger agencies. They're beholden to other agencies and talent sources to assemble the various elements in a movie.

Larger agencies are not as dependent. If you sign with an agent at one of the big agencies, movies can be assembled and packaged much easier, because the other important elements needed are already represented in-house. A hot blockbuster screenplay can attract a producer, director, and actors much quicker. The other benefit is that the agents at larger agencies tend to have more negotiating power. Their "talent bank" is much broader and bigger. This can give them a stronger bargaining position.

The negative side, for the beginning screenwriter, is a much smaller profile in the scheme of things. Rather than being the agent's sole focus, the beginning screenwriter becomes more of a peripheral figure in the overall development of the movie. At one of the larger agencies, especially, it's easy and quite common for a beginning screenwriter's interests to get lost in the movie-packaging shuffle.

Finding an agent of any kind is usually the sole objective for any beginning screenwriter. Even so, you should still focus your pursuit in a way that serves your best interests.

FINDING AN AGENT

The pursuit of an agent for a beginning screenwriter is usually a frustrating and wearying process of trying to get someone, anyone, to take a chance and believe that you have what it takes to be a screenwriter.

It will often feel like you're trying to sell something no one wants to buy.

It's rarely an easy achievement, and it's different for every screenwriter, but it's the way the game is played. It's a free-wheeling process where there are no real rules. You have to go out there and fight for what you want.

The first step is to assemble a list of agencies and agents you want to target in your efforts.

To best sources for doing this are:

THE HOLLYWOOD CREATIVE DIRECTORY–AGENTS AND MANAGERS This is the most comprehensive guide to agents and managers. It provides contact information (address, phone, fax, e-mail), along with other useful supplementary information (types of talent represented, union affiliations, etc.). You can purchase it in book form or subscribe to it online.

It's an excellent research source you can use to learn about the size and capabilities of the individual agencies and also which specific agents to target.

Phone: 310-315-4815/800-815-0503
Website: www.hcdonline.com

THE WRITER'S GUILD OF AMERICA, INC. The Writer's Guild publishes two listings that can be used.

The first is a Member Directory that lists each member's credits and identifies their agent or manager. If there's a particular genre or screenwriter you admire, this may be one way to start. You can look up the screenwriters who write in a specific genre and see who their agents are, or you can choose the screenwriters you admire.

But going after the agent of a top-level screenwriter is generally not advisable for someone just starting their career.

The Writer's Guild also publishes two lists of approved signatory agencies. These are general listings without much detail, but they insure that a listed agency adheres to an accepted level of professional behavior. These lists are the two best sources for agencies and how to contact them.

WGA, EAST
Phone: 212-767-7800
Website: www.wgaeast.org

WGA, WEST
Phone: 323-951-4000
Website: www.wga.org

But there's another source you should already have been using.

If you've taken courses, entered contests, gone to screenwriting events, and generally done anything and everything you can to network yourself and your work, then you should have already compiled some contacts.

These are people who are more on the inside than you are, however big or small that distance might be.

Remember that you want to be open and honest about your goals and dreams as a screenwriter. This is what you want to communicate to anybody who can be helpful or become a contact. This also includes asking about agents and learning as much as you can. While you should read the trades (*Variety* and *The Hollywood Reporter*) to stay up to date on the agency business, more specific and useful information will come from insiders you can talk to and ask to share their experiences.

Let's hope you will have also given your screenplay to people who have read it and loved it. Or that it's won a prize in a contest.

Or a friend, a relative, or teacher has sent it to someone they know in the industry, and they loved it, too.

Because here's the challenge you're facing: Agents work very hard for the clients they already have. As such, the sheer volume of requests that come in from new screenwriters is impossible to respond to in any kind of individual or thoughtful manner. By necessity, most agents will only respond to new screenwriters who are special in some way and can distinguish themselves from the mass of requests that pour in. There's just no way an agent could read even a fraction of the screenplays from new screenwriters. Plus, experience has proved that the overwhelming majority just aren't very good.

The strongest advantage is to have a recommendation from someone the agent knows, or a recommendation from someone in the industry. Anything that gives you a personal connection to the agent is one of the surest ways to break out of the crowd.

You also want to be able to distinguish your screenplay if you can. That's where contests can help. Winning a prize or recognition from a well-known screenwriting contest also gives you an advantage.

Just like blockbuster movies have to have a big idea to attract an audience, you have to figure out an effective way to attract an agent. It can be because of a personal connection, awards, distinctions, or anything else.

MAKING CONTACT WITH AN AGENT

Following are the traditional methods for approaching an agent.

Write a Query Letter

A query letter is a request sent to a specific agent seeking representation. It introduces you and describes the screenplay you'd like to be read as a sample of your writing talents. In simplest terms, a query letter is a way of attracting an agent's interest and getting your screenplay read. That's its primary goal. So everything in your letter should serve that purpose.

Follow the format of a business letter. Use good-quality white paper with your contact information (name, address, phone, fax, e-mail) in the letterhead. Don't use a fancy font. Courier or Times New Roman is best.

The letter should be no more than one page, single-spaced.

Write to a specific individual, not just the agency. This is essential. Your letter has to go to someone you've researched as being appropriate. Sending a query letter to the agency as a whole indicates a lack of diligence and professionalism. Even if you're not a professional yet, you should act like one—especially to the person you want to represent your professional services.

For the contents, just remember the goal of the letter: to hook the reader into wanting to read your screenplay.

Begin by personalizing the letter. If you have a personal connection, or have been recommended by someone, that's a good way to open. This will catch the agent's attention, which is what you want. Or you can specify why you've chosen this specific agent. Anything that shows your understanding of the agent's needs and expertise can also be a hook.

Or the best opening might be to use your screenplay itself to catch the agent's attention. Using a great log line or story hook can also be a terrific opening.

Whatever way you choose, it should grab the agent's interest right from the start.

After that, describe your movie story in the most vivid and powerful way possible. Not the plot, though. Zero in on what's blockbuster and unique about your screenplay. Communicate the essence of your story's appeal to an audience. Be short and concise. Sell the idea of your story, not the story itself. You want the agent to be hooked by your big idea and motivated to read your screenplay.

Finally, sell what's unique and special about you as a writer. Note any writing or filmmaking achievements and awards. The writing achievements don't have to be just screenwriting. If you're a produced playwright or published author, it supports your writing credentials. Also include your educational background if it's relevant (film school, etc.) Other life experiences can be effective to note here, too. If your screenplay is about a subject that comes out of your specialized knowledge or experiences, this is worth noting. The purpose of this paragraph is to introduce you as a writer in the same vivid and exciting way you described your screenplay.

At the end of the letter, ask if you can send the agent your screenplay. Be polite but clear about what you want.

You can include a self-addressed stamped envelope or postcard for a reply. Or you can specify a phone number to call if interested.

Use the letter itself to showcase your writing skills. It should be without any kind of errors, of course. But also use it to show the qualities your screenplay will have. Make your query letter funny, exciting, clever, or dramatic, depending on the genre of your screenplay. A boring or sloppily written query letter is worthless.

It's important to note, though, that query letters are becoming less effective because of the sheer volume mentioned before. As Emile Gladstone said in his interview, agents, especially the ones at the top agencies, are inundated beyond their desire and capabilities to respond. As such, success with a query letter is becoming increasingly difficult.

This is where research can help. Sending a query letter cold to a veteran agent without some kind of connection is a long shot at the very best. The better tactic is to target a new agent, or start with small agencies. You're hungry and ambitious to start your screenwriting career. A great query letter written to a hungry and ambitious agent starting his or her own career can be a great match.

When you begin sending out query letters, also keep a tracking system. Follow up with a phone call, even if you've included a self-addressed stamped letter or postcard.

Remember this, too: Always conduct yourself in a way that's pleasant and positive with everyone you deal with. The receptionist, secretary, or personal assistant you talk to is climbing the career-ladder, just like you. In a few years, he or she may be an agent, a development executive, or some other higher-level position. Build relationships and contacts with anyone you can.

The reverse is also true. The lower-level person should also realize that you just may be the next hot blockbuster screenwriter.

Call on the Phone

Like the query letter, calling an agent directly without an introduction is a long shot, but it's worked on occasion, so it's worth considering. (See how it worked for David Goyer in the Blockbuster Advice at the end of the chapter). The objective is the same as the query letter. You want to get an agent to read your screenplay.

Just as with the query letter, the odds are not in your favor, but that doesn't matter. All you need is one person to say yes, so you should try everything until you reach that person. The only sure way not to get an agent is to stop trying.

When you call, be prepared with the same information you included in your query letter. Say you're a new screenwriter looking for representation. Then describe your screenplay and state your credentials. How far you get, if at all, will vary, of course. Usually, you'll get a polite, but firm, reply from the receptionist or secretary stating that the agent doesn't accept unsolicited screenplays.

Then ask if there's anyone else at the agency who will read your work. This includes the receptionist or secretary you're talking to. Because if they read it and love it, they'll give it to a superior, and this could be the personal connection you're looking for.

Discovering a great screenplay is a benefit to whoever finds it. People at the beginning of their Hollywood careers are looking for ways to distinguish themselves, and going to their boss with a great screenplay is always a career booster.

Finding an agent is one of the more enigmatic and mysterious rites of passage for a beginning screenwriter. It's a big challenge, but one worth pursuing.

Before facing this challenge, though, don't forget a crucial fact. Getting to an agent is meaningless if the screenplay you send isn't first-rate. You have to work hard to get your screenplay to an agent, but your hard work is worthless if you don't have a great screenplay to show.

BLOCKBUSTER ADVICE

Agents

In the beginning, start looking for an agent in the ways just covered, but don't let that search be your primary focus. Be a writer. Write screenplays. Work hard on becoming what agents want, which is a screenwriter who can create stories that thrill millions.

SOME THOUGHTS ABOUT AGENTS

The screenwriters agree on the need to have an agent, but it's a business relationship that has to work for both sides to be successful.

NEAL BRENNAN *(Half Baked)*

What you have to remember about agents is that they're not family and they're not your friends. It's not like in the movies, where they pick you up out of the gutter and discover you, and encourage you, and there's a real personal connection.

Usually, it's a real capitalist relationship. I actually told my agent when I signed with her, "Look, I don't need your notes." Because I know more about writing movies than my agent does. I don't really care if my agent likes my material. Just sell it. That's what I need.

There's already enough rejection from everybody else. I just want my agent to help me. People want their egos gratified. I don't think that agents have better taste than anybody else. Look, I'm an authority on movies, and I'm an authority on screenwriting. Comedy, too. That's about it, but that's what I know.

PHILIP EISNER *(Event Horizon)*

I've been with the same agent my entire career. I was actually her first sale. She came from New York to Los Angeles and opened up a small agency. There are pluses and minuses to being with a small agency. You don't necessarily have the huge packaging weight that the big agencies have.

At the same time, I never worry about whether my agent is working for me. I know she only has a dozen or so clients, so she doesn't service a lot of people.

DAVID HAYTER *(X-Men)*

For me, my agents provide a relationship with the rest of the Hollywood community that I don't necessarily want to worry about. I don't want to have to go out to parties to find jobs. I prefer to live my quiet life and remain a mystery, which I think is a more attractive image.

ANDREW MARLOWE *(Air Force One)*

Ultimately, getting an agent is essential. Agents know where the jobs are. You can flail about for a long time doing blind submissions, but you're at the bottom of the pile, and nobody is reading you with any positive bias.

You're just another guy out there and you're competing against this avalanche of material that's being thrown at Hollywood. You need to do something to distinguish your material before they even get it.

Getting an Agent

The screenwriters acknowledge the difficulty of getting an agent, but also offer some good advice that supports the different methods we've identified.

There's no easy way to get an agent, especially at the very beginning of your career, but it's a challenge that's necessary to pursue.

DAVID BENIOFF *(The 25th Hour)*

Sadly enough, a lot of it is about using your connections. It's tough to just send things in cold. It'll end up in the slush pile. I do think it's really important to move to Los Angeles. Especially if you're a nobody. There are so many screenplays floating around, you need every advantage you can get. I wouldn't have gotten my first assignment if I wasn't living here.

PHILIP EISNER *(Event Horizon)*

I'm on the Writer's Guild mentor list and I'm always getting e-mails on how to get an agent. They say they have a great idea and need to get an agent. I always write back and tell them that they first need to think about being a good writer, not just having an idea.

DAVID GOYER *(Blade)*

In terms of getting an agent, you have to believe in your work. Most people are looking for a reason to say no.

Because as soon as they say yes, they're putting their reputation on the line. It's easier to say no. So there's a lot of people who will tell you that your screenplay is a bad idea, or it's a bad screenplay. So you absolutely have to believe in yourself.

I got an agent when I was still in film school. I got my agent by cold calling him. Over the course of a month, I called him eighteen times before he took my call. Finally he picked up the phone and said, "Who are you? Why are you calling me?" I said, "I'm going to be a really huge filmmaker and you're going to kick yourself if you don't read my script." I said it because I figured it couldn't hurt. I had nothing to lose.

Look, Hollywood is an industry that thrives on hubris, on showmanship. So even if you don't really have the talent to back it up, you have nothing to lose by saying you do. The worst they're going to say is, "No, you suck," or "You stink" or "Your writing is no good."

But you know what? They're going to say that to you anyway, even if your writing is great.

ANDREW MARLOWE (*Air Force One*)

I would encourage any beginning screenwriter who wants to get representation in Hollywood to enter the major contests. That's what worked for me. I won the Nicholl fellowship. Because if you're not placing in the highest levels of the screenwriting contests, you're probably not ready to make the leap to Hollywood. You probably need to work on your craft some more.

Another mistake beginning screenwriters make is trying to get the agent on the phone. They try to bypass the assistant to get to the agent. But the assistants are the ones with all the power. The agent is usually just going to be annoyed that you're wasting their time, because you're not one of their clients. They've got a million things to do, and you're asking them to give up two hours of their time on the weekend to read something they have no idea is any good.

But every assistant is looking for a way to move up the ladder. Talk to the agent's assistant just after lunch when the phone's aren't lighting up. Tell them about your script and why you think it's special. Ask them if they'll read it, and if they like it, pass it along to their boss. If the assistant loves it, they'll give it to their boss with a recommendation. So the boss will be pre-biased to like it. Assistants are the gate-keepers.

They have enormous power in Hollywood.

READERS AND DEVELOPMENT EXECUTIVES NEED LOVE

"There is no right and wrong.
There is only fun and boring."
—Hackers

Once an agent has agreed to represent your work, the next step is to submit it to the industry. Good agents will know which studios, producers, and production companies will most likely be interested in the kind of material your screenplay represents. Agents network the industry relentlessly, so they'll know the best match for your screenplay.

A key part of understanding the movie industry is understanding that some studios are more likely to take on certain kinds of projects than others. A small studio like Artisan doesn't have the resources to take on a large scale movie like *Gladiator*, but this might be exactly the kind of movie a big studio like Warner Bros. is looking for. It's a marketplace, and you have to know who will be interested in buying what you're selling.

The movie industry is swamped with thousands of screenplays (and other forms of creative material) constantly pouring into the system. And it really is a swamp for the people on the inside trying to figure out how to manage a way through the never-ending onslaught of pages and pages that have to be read.

Imagine that one of those screenplays, among all the hundreds and thousands of others, is yours .

How do you survive and succeed?

FIRST YOU MAKE LOVE TO A READER

That is, you have to write a screenplay a reader will fall in love with.

When an agent sends a screenplay out to a studio or production company, the first stop is usually with "a reader."

A reader, or story analyst, is generally someone at the beginning of his or her career. All have aspirations to be a producer, a screenwriter, the president of a studio, or ascend to some other high level job. Readers are usually smart. They may have an Ivy League diploma or a Ph.D. in eighteenth century French literature. They're there because they all love movies, just like you do.

A reader's job is to read submitted screenplays and write "coverage." Coverage is a short summation, and analysis of a screenplay, with a specific recommendation on whether it should be considered for purchase.

The big studios and most production companies all use readers. It's a demanding and often wearying job. The goal, of course, is to find the screenplay diamond that's hidden away in the flood of incoming scripts.

Like agents, readers will also be judging your screenplay on it's professionalism and story-telling skills. If your screenplay is sloppy or poorly conceived in any way, that's reason enough for the reader to give it a "pass." Your screenplay has to be superior for a reader to pull it out of the pile and give it a "consider."

But it's an industry reality that most of these screenplays aren't very good. Actually, to be more clear, most of them are *very, very not good*. So it's not an impossible task at all to capture a reader's attention with a great script.

What readers respond to most of all is that word that keeps popping up . . .

NEW.

Because readers read so many screenplays, they're quick to reject all the generic stories that have been done over and over. That's why it's so important that you know "the world of stories" and have a big idea.

Blockbuster movies always aspire to be a step in a bigger or different direction from what's already been done.

This especially includes anything that's been the flavor-of-the-month, or the hot-new-thing, because it invariably brings on a wave of wanna-bes who mimic the original without adding anything new. Don't bring them a Quentin Tarantino-style script, because that's what *he* writes. Don't submit a Charlie Kaufman-style script, because that's what *he* writes.

Readers are always turned off by a screenplay that's just an unoriginal echo of an idea or a story style that's been done before.

The best way to win over a reader with your screenplay is with a story that shocks, surprises, startles, and grabs them with a concept that's new and different.

Readers love movies and great stories, or they wouldn't be where they are.

DEVELOPMENT EXECUTIVES NEED LOVE, TOO

When a screenplay reaches a development executive, it's higher up the hill, but there's still a ways to go.

If you want your screenplay to keep climbing, then the development executive has to love it, too.

Development executives are generally mid-level at a studio or production company. It's their job to seek out and find suitable screenplays for the company to acquire. This can also involve optioning plays, books, or other forms of dramatic material for adaptation. While the reader's job is to evaluate screenplays, the development executive is more actively engaged in selecting screenplays to be bought for the company. When this is done, the development executive also works with the screenwriter, "developing" the screenplay. This means revising and polishing the screenplay with the company's creative input.

At this point, your screenplay is usually assumed to be at least a moderately professional effort. What development and production executives are then looking at is if this movie-project is right for their company.

All companies buy screenplays based on a variety of business-related elements: budgets, type of story, what's already in development, what actors and directors they have relationships with, etc.

So you may have written the greatest screenplay in the world, but it may not be the right fit for one reason or another. If the production company is run by an actor or a director, then the development person is obviously guided by the needs and creative sensibilities of whoever that is.

At this point, the people reading your script are also probably more experienced and knowledgeable about the high-stakes gamble of commercial movie-making. They've lived the victories and defeats more personally, so they're more attuned to the market place. They're more aware of which kinds of movies have done well and which haven't. While the search is always for new stories, recent box-office history is a factor, too.

Development executives start every day with the hope that they'll read a terrific screenplay they can recommend to the higher-ups who have to bet the big money. If you want that screenplay to be yours, then you have a goal, too.

You have to write a screenplay they love.

STUDIO EXECUTIVES HAVE TO HIT IT BIG

*"I don't care about the money.
I'm pulling back the curtain.
I want to meet the wizard."*
—The Game

In any movie company or studio, it comes down to one or more people who have the ability to finally say "yes" to your screenplay. It's this person's decision that determines which screenplays to buy and for how much.

The best situation is if more than one company wants your screenplay, because then it becomes a bidding war that drives up the price. If it's a great blockbuster script, that price can quickly reach $1 million and more.

IT'S A BIG JOB BECAUSE OF BIG DECISIONS

Being a top studio executive is one of the most powerful jobs in the movie business, but it's also one of the most intensely pressurized and volatile. It's a high-pressure job because it means making the decisions that will literally define the future success of the company. It's a job where a roll of the dice on which movie to make can mean millions and millions of dollars.

Either won or lost.

Imagine it yourself.

Pretend for a moment it's your job to pick the stories that will be the movies for the company you run. It's your decision and yours alone. Imagine you're sitting at your desk reading through the stack of screenplays that have been recommended by your development executives.

The first one you read is about a famous ocean liner that hits an iceberg and hundreds of people die.

The second one is about a colossal pre-historic creature that terrorizes Manhattan.

The third one you read is based on a comic book about a secret government agency that monitors alien creatures who are living in disguise on Earth.

Let's say you love all three. The screenplays are great. They've all got spectacular action, daredevil thrills, a great heart-tugging love story, and a main character you can identify with and root for. You think they'd all make terrific movies and be box-office hits.

You're right, of course, because they all were.

In fact, I'm sure you already know what they are, and probably saw all three.

The movies are *Titanic*, *Godzilla* and *Men in Black*.

All were smash hits and made tons of money for the studios that produced them. All three had long and complicated paths to the screen. But they finally got there because a studio executive believed in the project. In all three cases though, the executive could have bet wrong. You never know until the audience makes it's decision, too.

By the way, if you're still pretending you're the studio executive, here's the other piece of the puzzle that's part of your job. Remember, you're betting big money on whether you're right or wrong. This is how much it cost to produce each movie (prints and advertising not included):

• TITANIC — $200 MILLION

• GODZILLA — $125 MILLION

• MEN IN BLACK — $90 MILLION

This is why blockbuster movies have to attract a huge audience. The growing economics of making big movies puts very specific demands on the kind of stories that are told. They have to be terrifically entertaining and skillfully told audience-pleasers.

If you're still pretending to be a studio executive, ask yourself this question: Would you spend $100 million on a story you loved, but you weren't sure other people would?

Studio executives look at blockbuster screenplays in a very specific way. Is it a great story? That's always the first consideration. But there's always a bigger question.

Is this a story millions of people will want to see?

Let's say there's another screenplay you take off the pile. It's a story about the Vikings in A.D. 922 and how an Arab helps them fight a mysterious band of flesh-eating creatures. Maybe you love this screenplay, too. You think it's got all the key ingredients for a hit. It's also based on a book by a mega-selling novelist whose books have been made into some of the most successful movies of all time.

So you decide to go for it.

Well, this time you bet wrong.

The movie is *The 13th Warrior,* adapted from the novel *Eaters of the Dead,* by Michael Crichton. It starred Antonio Banderas and was directed by John McTiernan, the director of *Die Hard* and *Predator.* It cost $125 million to produce and it only grossed $41.9 million at the box office.

That's a loss of $83.1 million.

The fact that economics play such an important part in movie-making is just a fact of life. With the enormous costs involved, studio executives have to make movies that hit it big with the audience—or they won't be in business very long.

THEY BOUGHT IT ONCE, SO THEY'LL BUY IT AGAIN

To the outside observer, these decisions may often seem silly and dumb. The attitude of many screenwriters is to bemoan the crassness of the powers that be. The truth is, for the most part, studio executives and producers are simply trying to figure out what audiences want to see. That's pretty much it. Sure, they want to make great movies, but they have to be movies that bring in an audience.

So studio executives use what they know, which are the inarguable facts of the marketplace. Here's a list of the top twenty grossing movies of all time:

1. *Titanic*
2. *Star Wars*
3. *E.T.*
4. *Star Wars: The Phantom Menace*
5. *Spiderman*
6. *Jurassic Park*
7. *The Lord of the Rings: The Two Towers*
8. *Forrest Gump*
9. *The Lion King*
10. *Harry Potter and the Sorcerer's Stone*
11. *The Lord of the Rings: The Fellowship of the Ring*
12. *Star Wars: Attack of the Clones*
13. *Star Wars: Return of the Jedi*
14. *Independence Day*
15. *The Sixth Sense*
16. *Star Wars: The Empire Strikes Back*
17. *Home Alone*
18. *Shrek*
19. *Harry Potter and the Chamber of Secrets*
20. *Jaws*

As this is being written in 2003, these are the biggest blockbuster movies of all time. That means every major producer and studio executive in Hollywood can recite the list from memory, along with the next ten, and the next ten, and can probably give you the opening weekend grosses down to the dollar.

But this short list should in no way suggest that you have to write this kind of movie. That would just be mimicking the marketplace and foolish; instead you want to understand the marketplace and use your creativity to write your own great stories.

Just keep in mind the broad qualities of blockbuster movies we've already talked about and are clearly evident in the above list.

They have spectacle. There's nothing humdrum or boring about any of the top-grossing movies. Most are sweeping panoramic stories with stunning visuals, great action, and glorious imagination. Each, in their own way, is mythic in scale and purpose.

They're about basic human values. Underneath all the big screen bells and whistles, the stories are also about the fundamental issues of life. They're about characters finding true love, searching for their purpose in life, trying to stay alive and conquering whatever soul-changing challenges stand in their way.

They're genre movies. For the most part, the above movies can also be considered genre movies. Great ones, of course. They deliver big-time on all the time-honored story elements and entertainment thrills audiences love and expect from these kinds of stories. They give the audience what they want with big-screen flair and style.

David Goyer is normally known for his urban, gothic-toned action movies like *Blade*, *Dark City* and *Crow: City of Angels*. In the following, he reveals how a desire to write in a different genre led to a million dollar sale.

FROM IDEA TO MILLION DOLLAR $ALE

David Goyer

The screenplay, *Evermere*, is a rousing fantasy epic about a young boy's journey to a parallel world where he discovers his true identity. It's a wildly imaginative story packed with heroes, rogues, dark magic, evil trolls, dwarves, and lots of other magical creatures and fantastic landscapes.

The movie hasn't been made yet, but the screenplay remains one of the more legendary million dollar spec screenplay sales.

Evermere began as a spec script I started writing myself. I wanted do something that was more like a fairy tale or a fable than the material I'd been writing. I finished about forty pages of it and got stuck. I decided to ask a friend of mine, James Robinson, who's a comic-book writer, if he wanted to collaborate on it. He did.

When we finished, our agent, Phil Raskind at Endeavor, thought it was a big enough film we could send it to everyone at once. It's called "shotgunning." We went out to the studios on a Friday. We were expecting to hear back from people on Monday at the earliest.

But on Saturday, Andy Vanja tracked down my agent, who was in Palm Springs for the weekend. My agent called me at home and said

Andy and his partner Mario Kassar wanted to make a pre-emptive bid. With a pre-emptive bid, you're gambling that another bid won't come in that's higher.

Their bid was for $1.25 million against $2.5 million. That started four hours of back and forth negotiations until about 12:30 that night. It was definitely exciting. We ended up taking the offer.

In the following interview, one of the best young studio executives in Hollywood gives her views on many of the issues facing a beginning screenwriter, including what will excite and thrill her in a spec screenplay.

What beginning screenwriters have to realize is that the people they want to buy their screenplay love movies as much as they do, but their role in the process is very different. Studio executives have a single, very clearly defined job responsibility, and that's to make hit movies.

Stokely Chaffin is the senior vice-president of development and production at New Line Cinema. Her most current project is executive producing *Freddy Vs. Jason,* which is scheduled for release summer/fall 2003. Before joining New Line, she was a highly respected producer and development executive involved with movies such as *Volcano, I Know What You Did Last Summer* and *Sweet Home Alabama.* She began her career at Neal Moritz's Original Films in 1993 after graduating from Harvard.

I love popcorn movies that are escapist, that you go to on a Friday night because you want to have fun. And I work at a company that was built on genre pictures. That's horror, action, thrillers, and comedies. New Line basically got its start from *Nightmare On Elm Street. Freddy Vs. Jason* is a new project I'm working on, and it's an example of the kind of movie I like to make. It's a very commercial idea that a good filmmaker can make special.

So my personal taste and the company I work at are very attracted to genre stories. Are they always the best movies out there? Probably not. Maybe *Ice Storm* and *Adaptation* will have more critical acclaim. But they're not the kind of movies the biggest audiences want to see. And they're not the kind of movies that make a lot of money. We're a business, and we're in the business of making money.

It's about finding a strong central idea and making it in the smartest way possible. It's not about having contempt for making popcorn movies or really mainstream, commercial movies. It's about trying to find a fresh idea that maybe in some ways is a formula, but you figure out a way to do it in a different way.

The most critical element in any screenplay is its central idea. It doesn't have to be high-concept, but it has to be strong. It has to be the kind of idea that if you tell it to somebody in one sentence they get excited. To me, the central idea is absolutely the most important part of a screenplay. People are looking for an idea they can get excited about. There's a lot of material out there. It takes a great idea to be separated from the rest of them.

I will buy a bad screenplay that has a great idea. I will buy a bad pitch that has a great idea. In fact, most of my slate of fifteen movies that I've bought in the last year or so didn't start out as the best source material. But I knew it could be fixed. You know that you can bring in a writer that can execute and optimize the idea.

I'll always respond to a screenplay when it's clear the person is just a great writer. A lot of the great writers are people who are wonderful with language, have obviously read a lot, and are smart. That is really meaningful. It does matter when somebody knows how to write a beautiful sentence. When you're reading a script on a Sunday afternoon and you get to the one that's really well-written, it totally jumps out of the pile. It may not get your screenplay sold, but it always helps.

When something is beautifully written, you just feel like you're in good hands. You still might not like the story, but you might want to go back to that person later with something else.

That's what happened with *Sweet Home Alabama*, a movie I produced. I read a script written by C. Jay Cox that I loved. It took place in the South. It was funny and wild. It had amazing characters and some of the most beautiful language you could imagine. But it wasn't a story I could get made. So I brought him in to work on the screenplay to *Sweet Home Alabama*. We worked on it for a couple of years before we sold it as a pitch.

If you can't come up with a big idea that a studio will love, that can be okay, too. If you have a great story to tell, and it's smaller and more personal, then you should probably go ahead and write it. A studio almost definitely won't buy it, but it may get you noticed, and that's what you want.

A lot of beginning screenwriters will keep their ideas very close to their vest and that's a mistake. They get scared somebody is going to steal their idea. But you shouldn't underestimate producers. Part of their job is to get in a room with you, kick story ideas around, and work them out. The bottom line is you have to share your ideas to sell them.

Also be professional. Learn the format. If you open a script and there's something wrong with the format, you already think you're not in good hands. It can definitely hurt.

I'll buy a screenplay from anybody, an ogre, I don't care. I really don't. But if I'm going to be working closely with a writer in the development process, the personality does play a role. You want somebody that listens to you, but doesn't do everything you say. You want somebody who hopefully respects your brain, but you also have to earn that.

But mainly, you want somebody who won't defend their original idea until the death. They have to be willing to listen to what you think the problem is, then come up with a better solution than the one you may have. They can't be defensive about the collaboration process.

I spend so much of my time with slick agents and other people. When you get into a room with a writer, it's usually a joy. Most of the time, they're just incredibly interesting, quirky, and intelligent people. Slick is what most writers aren't, and that's great.

You don't have to live in Los Angeles when you write your first screenplay. But if your first script is good, and it helps you get an agent, then you've got to help that agent introduce you to the people who can hire you. You can keep writing spec screenplays wherever you are, but if one sells, it's easier to be here for meetings. In the beginning, especially, it's super-helpful.

Honestly, don't try to reinvent the wheel. Try to find a genre that you love and really be smart about filling that universe with interesting new people we've never seen. Try to find a really fresh idea that works within a proven formula or genre.

If you write a great script, you can't keep it from getting to the right people. There are so many hungry assistants and development people who are actively searching for great scripts, all you have to do is write one. A great screenplay will get noticed.

And it absolutely does not matter if you're a beginner. It doesn't matter in the least. In fact, it's sometimes better, because the producer or studio knows they can get the story for a reasonable amount of money. It can actually be a plus.

IN THE HOLLYWOOD MOVIE GAME, BE A PLAYER

Being a successful screenwriter entails much more than just being able to write a great screenplay. Understanding what the other players want is an equally important skill.

The chapters in this section have shown what your screenplay has to go through to be marketed in the Hollywood system and be bought. Knowing what excites agents, readers, development executives, and studio executives, is how you do this. What you want most of all is for your screenplay to land anonymously on somebody's desk and, when they pick it up, no matter what time of day it is, what else they have on their mind, or how many screenplays they've already read that day, they open yours and begin reading what you've written, and the words on the page gradually begin to disappear as they turn the pages faster and faster, because another world is coming into view, the amazing new world of your story.

And it's astonishing.

Working with Studio Executives

Because studio executives are the ultimate gatekeepers who decide which movies will get made, blockbuster screenwriters write stories that have to meet the needs and demands of the studio system. It's a fact of life, given the various economic reasons we've already talked about.

It can be frustrating and difficult for the screenwriter, as the following will reveal. But smart screenwriters learn how to operate effectively within this system and protect their creative visions.

DAVID BENIOFF *(The 25th Hour)*

I think it's really important for screenwriters coming to Hollywood to read something about the town. There are several really good books about Hollywood. They should try to get rid of some of those illusions before they come out here. Because it is a business. You have to understand that the studio executives are not getting promotions and keeping their jobs based on satisfying screenwriters, or coming up with good art movies. They need to make money. I think understanding the reality of the business is important.

You'd like to believe that you write a script and if a producer or studio loves the script, they'll try to get the best possible director for it. But what happens a lot of time is they get who the studio has a deal with, or who politically they owe a favor to. And that can happen a lot of times with casting, too. This person might be perfect for the role, but they're tied up for the next three years. You very rarely get to put the perfect pieces together. It's just reality.

NEAL BRENNAN *(Half Baked)*

Your personality is immeasurably important; I can't say enough about it. The way they hire people at individual studios is from a list. I'm on the comedy list. What will happen is they will send you an idea or something to rewrite and you have to pitch them your take. So you have to go in and sell them; you have to be a persuasive force. You can't go in and sort of mumble your way through it. You have to be enthusiastic. You have to sell them.

PHILIP EISNER *(Event Horizon)*

There's something that's important to distinguish between producers and studio executives. Producers get paid if a movie is made. Studio executives get fired if a movie goes into production and doesn't do well. So the two are actually working at cross purposes. The producer is doing everything he can to get the studio to say "yes," and the studio executive is doing everything he can to say "no."

This is how it affects the process. The studio wants to make commercial movies, and the producers want the studio executives to be happy, so they'll do what the studio wants. The producers are practical. Writers are more story oriented. That's where the creative differences often occur.

As a screenwriter, you need to cultivate a little bit of Zen in your life. Because it's not going to be about you. At some point, it's not going to be about the story. It becomes about the business and the necessities of the business. If you really want it to be about you and your craft, then you should write novels.

AKIVA GOLDSMAN *(A Beautiful Mind)*

One is always tempted to find a "them," the person or people who are responsible for why things are bad. And I really wish there was a "them" because it would imply a level of organization that I think doesn't exist.

Mostly, you just have folks who are guessing, just like you

are, and they've guessed successfully more often than not. That's why the top producers and studio executives are generally better, because they've moved further along.

But nobody has it figured out completely. Making a movie is a really impossible process. It's a coalescence of little miracles. If anybody had it nailed, they'd be batting a thousand.

DAVID GOYER (Blade)

It's always a risk to make a movie, so studio executives are looking for a reason to bet on you. Everybody wants to feel safe. They want to feel there's a certain amount of confidence, or a certain amount of hubris in the writer of the material. So if you project that confidence and make it easier about buying your script, that's really helpful.

Studio executives are terrified of failing. They have to feel confident in the writer and the screenplay. They want to be able to come into a meeting and say, "This is genius." Even if you're not well known, they want to say, "This kid is a genius. This kid is going to make us a hundred million dollars."

Studio executives tend to boil movie ideas down into one-sheets. They want to know how they can sell it with a log line on a movie poster. They want to know they can get butts in the seats. That's where the whole high-concept craze came from.

What's funny about everything that's happened with the *Blade* movies is they've now become something that other movies and TV shows refer to. It's become one of those influential franchises. But when we were working on the first *Blade* movie, which came out well before *The Matrix*, people were saying, "You're going to combine Hong Kong action with vampires and black exploitation?" They didn't get it. They thought we were crazy.

Anytime something comes out that's fresh and new, it almost immediately becomes the status quo and nobody remembers that it was fresh and new to begin with.

DAVID HAYTER *(X-Men)*

For young screenwriters, my advice is to understand that the studio's business is not to make great movies, it's to make money. That's how they stay alive and that's how we as the creative element continue to work.

So I will sell a movie to a studio based on how much audience it's going to bring in, because I know that's their interest, and I try to meet that. Then, once the picture is on its way to production, I don't feel strapped down by commercial necessity. It doesn't hamper my imagination at all.

Having confidence in your work is very valuable in getting a job and keeping a job. What a producer or studio wants from a writer is for someone to come in and say, "Don't worry, I have you taken care of. I have ultimate confidence in what I'm going to do. In the end, you're going to be happy and you're going to be successful." That's my job. My job is to have everybody stop worrying about the script, because I'm going to give them what they want.

I come in and say, "Look, I know what I'm doing. I'm going to give you something and it's going to have great quality to it. In the places where you're not confident, we'll keep working until we're both satisfied—you on a commercial level, me on a creative level." And that's what they want. They genuinely want you to take responsibility.

Some studio executives are not very bright. You'll run into that from time to time. And it can be very frustrating when you feel like you're genuinely putting out ideas that are original and exciting, but they can't grasp it. The bad studio executive is completely reliant on movies they've seen in the past, and if you can't reference those, you'll never get your ideas across.

Studios don't want their big budget action movies too complicated. They don't mind if they're good, but they don't want the intricacy to get in the way of commercial viability. There's a certain need to sell to middle America, and I think studio executives don't give that segment of the population that much credit.

DALE LAUNER *(My Cousin Vinny)*

Most development people and studio executives don't know how to talk to screenwriters. So many times I'll be in a situation when somebody will say something, and I will hate them. I've left meetings where I've fantasized about slipping under an executive's car and snipping their brake-lines.

Some executives don't have common sense when dealing with screenwriters. You can see they start getting uncomfortable and squirmy because they want to tell you something bad about your script, and they don't know how to say it. So they soft-pedal it in a way that's worse. I'd rather somebody just came out and told me how they felt when they read certain parts of the story. If you don't like a character, tell me why. If there's no emotions attached to something, it has no value.

ANDREW MARLOWE *(Air Force One)*

A segment of studio executives are just in the business for the power, to hang out with movie stars. They're into the glitter. They're more interested in the deal than making the movie. There are a lot of them who love movies, but they're walking a fine line between telling a good story and getting a good return on their investment.

So when they're tossing out ideas, they're usually not serving the story, they're serving what they think the audience will want to see—which is why you end up with movies that play toward the cliché, toward the archetype and the happy ending. Because they know with a happy ending they'll make money.

SCOTT ROSENBERG *(Con Air)*

Your personality is incredibly important. You always have to walk the line between arrogance and confidence. Here's a true story. They were really high on this writer. They thought he was excellent, they loved this kid's work. But they always want to meet you. You can't carve out a career forever in Des Moines without going to Los Angeles. They always just want to see you.

So they flew this kid in to sell a pitch. But they ended up not hiring him because he was so unbelievably shy.

It's a very important quality to be strong in a room. I think if you can go in there and give them assurance, it's essential. They have to believe in you.

ED SOLOMON *(Men in Black)*

Studio executives need some kind of frame of reference with new ideas. It can be other successful movies or your own experiences as a writer if you're successful. They need some context for your idea.

It's very, very difficult for any kind of executive to to take an original, unique idea and sell it to their bosses without being able to say, "It's an interesting idea and it's a bit off, but it's written by so-and-so, who wrote something successful. Or you don't know the writer but it's an idea that's like something else that worked."

And it's not their fault. It's the nature of the system. It's extremely difficult to do that job.

If I want a job, then I go in completely confident. Because why should they pay me money if I don't know I can do it. And they need to feel confident. But if I'm not sure I want to do something or not, I'll say, "I'm not sure this is going to work. Let me take a shot and see if it will." Then if I do think it's going to work, you'll get a different me. Then I'll say, "This is what this needs to be."

I'll do production rewrites for people. You go in right before production. The studio's movie is a mess, they're scared, and they're looking for you to tell them why it's not working. Those are high paid jobs and high pressure jobs. When I take those kinds of jobs, I'll be certain I know what needs to be done. I won't take the job unless I do, because it's too much pressure.

But screenwriters and studio executives think about stories very differently. It's similar to the way parents and "Johns" think about hookers. Parents think of them as children who were once in their arms and grew up. Johns think of how they can use them for their own needs. If you're paid money for your work, the people who pay the money correctly feel they have the right to do whatever they want with it, and unfortunately, that's the truth I think.

Every movie I've worked on has been diminished by the process. It's just the nature of what happens. It's not because all the people are assholes, or idiots, because they're not. Some are, but not all. There are good people in the studio system. But the process makes it a rare exception that the film turns out better than the script.

HOW TO THINK
LIKE A HOLLYWOOD
SCREENWRITER

*"Do you think there's life out there?
If not, it seems like an awful
waste of space."*
—Contact

What the preceding chapters on Hollywood show is the career value of knowing what the Hollywood gatekeepers and buyers want from a blockbuster screenplay.

Sure, you can trust your instincts and only follow your inner muse as you write a screenplay that's uninfluenced by anything other than your own brilliant writing talent. And that screenplay might even sell for a million dollars.

But that's the hard way, not the smart way.

In a business that's so ruled by economics, it makes you a better screenwriter if you understand the business.

Agents, development people, producers, and studio executives all have a role to play. They all make decisions that determine which screenplays are pushed through the system and turned into movies. So if you're serious about being a successful screenwriter, you need to understand how their job affects yours. It's really that simple. The more you understand why decisions are made, the smarter you'll be as a screenwriter.

STUDY WHAT HOLLYWOOD IS BUYING

One of the best ways to gain insight into how the business works is to study what screenplays are being bought and developed. This is extremely helpful to beginning screenwriters, because it gives you a sense of what kinds of stories the industry is responding to.

First, you'll make sure you're not writing an idea that's already being done. It will also hone your instincts about what's a commercial movie idea. You'll see what's being done and that gives you a broad overview of what studios and production companies are buying.

Finally, by seeing what's being developed, you can then use your own talents to venture off in a new direction and write something fresh and different.

The following media sources are all highly recommended.

VARIETY, THE HOLLYWOOD REPORTER Both publications track the business of the entertainment industry. There's always a wealth of ongoing movie news and information. You can learn which screenplays are being bought; what's in development; what studios, producers, directors, and actors are involved; etc.

They mostly cover the high-profile activity. If you want to know about the business of blockbuster mainstream movies, this is where you start.

WWW.SCRIPTSALES.COM There's all kinds of helpful screenwriting information and advice on this site. Most importantly though, it's the home of *Done Deal*, which is a comprehensive listing of weekly screenplay sales, pitches, and high-profile assignments.

WWW.HOLLYWOODLITSALES.COM This is another excellent and wide-ranging site for screenwriting news and information. It also tracks spec screenplay sales, with a historical database available.

This site has the deepest sales-tracking information. For a beginning blockbuster screenwriter, it's the Library of Congress.

WWW.CORONA.BC.CA/FILMS Lots of news and information here, too. *Coming Attractions* is a great up-to-date listing of movie projects in development, ranging from those dying a slow death in development hell to those roaring down the fast-track to green-light heaven.

STAY UP-TO-DATE ON SCREENWRITING

Along with the above, screenwriters should also read the various screenwriting magazines that are available.

They give sales information and writing advice, too, but in a much more writer-friendly environment. There are also longer and more in-depth articles about craft, career building, and every other nook and cranny of the screenwriting process.

There are also always interviews with screenwriters, who talk about their experiences with the movies they wrote. This is behind-the-scenes stuff that gives the real deal about the screenwriter's highs and lows on the bumpy road to the big screen.

The screenwriting magazines have just become popular in the last decade or so. Read them. They're on your side. The best are *Creative Screenwriting*, *Scr(i)pt* and *Fade-In*.

Selling a screenplay is an uphill battle, but it can be a lot easier if you don't ignore the other people on the hill and you try to understand what they're fighting for, too. From the outside, the movie industry looks like a giant complicated contraption that's formidable, inscrutable, and damned hard to break into.

But there's a key that gets you inside.

A great screenplay with a big idea.

All the gatekeepers and buyers, the agents, the readers, the development people, the studio, they're all looking for the same thing. They're looking for a story that's new, amazing, and astonishing, because that's what they all have to find to make a movie that will bring millions of people to the movie theater.

When you start writing your screenplay, always remember the audience for your movie begins with the people in the industry who will read it first.

MORE TACTICS AND STRATEGIES

As a creative person, you can also be creative in how you market your screenplay.

Following is another tactic that can also be effective in getting your screenplay where it needs to be.

GO DIRECTLY TO THE MOVIE-MAKERS

This strategy involves getting your screenplay to the other key elements in the movie-making process. Producers, directors, and actors are always on the lookout for exciting new material, so it's possible to go directly to them with your screenplay.

With the flood of material pouring into agents, some power-brokers suggest this course of action as a better way to go. (See the interview with agent Emile Gladstone in chapter 16). Plus, having a producer, director, or actor with a proven box-office record attached to your screenplay greatly enhances its studio appeal.

With this tactic, too, research and understanding the marketplace is critical. First, you have to zero in on what kind of screenplay you've written. What's the genre? What's the budget? What are the lead acting roles? Then you have to use your understanding of the marketplace to determine which producers, directors, and actors will be the best fit for your movie story.

If you've written a big-budget, high-concept, mega-star action movie, then Joel Silver and Jerry Bruckheimer are two producers you should definitely pursue, along with John McTiernan and Tony Scott as directors. There are many other possibilities, too, and your research will identify who they are.

Don't send it to Merchant and Ivory as producers; that would be a mistake—or to Todd Solondz as a director, another mistake.

Don't send Wes Craven a slapstick comedy.

Don't send the Farrelly Brothers a beautifully written prison story, unless it has the guards and the prisoners doing some very funny stuff.

Most producers and directors have a specific kind of material they respond to. That's who you want to pursue. Get your screenplay to any producer, director, or actor who's career has already shown they love the kind of story you've written.

But also don't be too strict and rigid with this selection, either. Producers, directors, and actors are also looking for material that stretches their talents and expands their marketability. Directors and producers may be known for a certain kind of material, but they also look for variety and new opportunities. Actors, too. An actor may be pigeon-holed as a light comedian and want to appear in something edgier and with more high energy. An action star may want to show he can carry a romantic comedy.

The process you use to get your screenplay to a producer, director, or actor is generally the same as for an agent. You send a query letter or call directly. Again, be friendly and positive in all your dealings.

The Hollywood Creative Directory Series

As noted in the section on agents, this publication is a great source for research and contact information. The individual publications each focus on one profession. The publisher can be reached at:

Phone: 323-308-3490/800-815-0503
Website: www.hcdonline.com

HCD–AGENTS AND MANAGERS In addition to researching agents, you can also use this edition to find out which agencies and managers represent the producer, director, or actor you want to submit your screenplay to.

HCD–PRODUCERS This edition focuses on producers, from the biggest (studios, television networks) to the smallest. Many directors and actors have their own production company, so this is a way to contact them, also. Over 1,750 companies and over 9,000 producers, studios, and network executives are listed.

HCD–FILM DIRECTORS Contact and other useful information for directors. Includes directors of major studio feature films, independent films, foreign films, documentaries, animated films, made-for-TV films, and cable films. Over 4,000 directors listed.

HCD–FILM ACTORS Contact and other useful information for actors. Includes actors in major studio films, independent films, made-for-TV films and cable films. Over 6,000 actors listed.

DIRECTOR'S GUILD–MEMBER DIRECTORY This publication lists contact information and credits for directors. You can also call the Director's Guild directly and request the contact information for specific directors.

Los Angeles
Phone: 310-289-2000

New York
Phone: 212-581-0370
Website: www.dga.org

As you do when contacting agents, don't start at the top of the company or stop trying when you get your first "no." The best tactic is usually to deal with a junior executive or assistant. Be honest and enthusiastic about the purpose of your letter or call. A higher level executive is always less willing to accept a screenplay from an unknown writer. But someone starting out will be more open to taking a shot at reading your screenplay. If they love it, then it will get passed up the ladder to the producer, director or actor you want to reach.

FIGHT THE GOOD FIGHT

All blockbuster screenwriters have a collection of war stories and battle scars they've accumulated during their careers. These are the victories and defeats they've experienced along the way. It's an unavoidable part of the movie-making game.

Because movies are such a collaborative effort, and the stakes are so high, confrontations, disagreements, and compromises can occur at every stage.

As a beginning screenwriter, you have to be as bold and imaginative with starting your career as you are in your writing. There will be unreturned phone calls, broken promises, rejections, and all the other minor defeats and frustrations a beginning screenwriter endures. So you have to be your own hero and champion.

When you first start out, be assertive and steadfast about getting what you write out into the marketplace.

Then you have to keep trying and trying, because you believe in yourself and your writing.

No matter where you start out, or who you are, if you have the determination and the talent, your dreams can reach those giant glowing screens.

There will be dissapointment and obstacles every step along the way, but if you love the movies and have what it takes, you can do it. You can be your own movie hero.

Good luck as your journey begins.

257

A BLOCKBUSTER LIFE

Being a blockbuster screenwriter is one of the most exciting and challenging creative jobs there is. Here are some final thoughts on both the highs and lows of life as a million dollar screenwriter.

NEIL BRENNAN *(Half Baked)*

As an unknown writer, you feel like a complete leper and an idiot. You're talked down to constantly, if you're even talked to at all. But once you've sold a screenplay, all that changes, because people have no idea where screenplays come from. All they know is there are people who can write them, and now you're officially one of those people. You become sort of a witch doctor, a magical shaman.

AKIVA GOLDSMAN *(A Beautiful Mind)*

I enjoy all of it, and struggle with all of it, and sometimes revile all of it. It's my job. I have the best job in the world. I love it. I wouldn't trade it for any other job. But it's still a job.

DAVID GOYER *(Blade)*

There's nothing more fun than screening a movie you're proud of and having the audience connect with it in the way you intended. When the audience laughs at a joke you wrote, or is scared by something you created, at the end of the day, there's nothing more satisfying than that.

DAVID HAYTER *(X-Men)*

I love the business. I love it all. I love making the deal. I love writing. I love the meetings. I love being on set, the cables and the cameras. Writing screenplays is, so far in my experience, the greatest way to make a lot of money that I've ever encountered. It's quite wonderful. But at the same time, it can be quite painful. I think I'll feel more creatively fulfilled as a director, but I've certainly been compensated very well as a writer.

JIM KOUF *(Rush Hour)*

Screenwriting is a strange process, because it changes so radically. In the beginning, you're the most important person there is. It's all up to you to create the story. But once the screenplay is finished, your importance is over. Everybody else takes over and you're basically forgotten. It takes some getting used to.

DALE LAUNER *(My Cousin Vinny)*

What I hate about the business is that screenwriters can come up with a story, then turn that story into a screenplay, populate it with characters, put in the motivation for each character, create everything they say, along with every subplot, every set-up, every pay off, every twist and turn, from beginning to end, and the director gets all the credit for it.

ANDREW MARLOWE *(Air Force One)*

Because of *Air Force One* and *End of Days* I get $1 million to $1.5 million a script now. But money ends up being a trap, too. If they're paying you a million dollars, you're looking at the pages thinking, is this worth a million dollars? It can handcuff you. It can make you really uncomfortable. It does affect the creative process. You want to write without self-editing yourself. But what happens is you keep asking yourself if what you wrote is worth a million dollars.

On the other side of the coin, I wake up every day incredibly thankful that I'm able to do what I do and get paid for it. I feel fortunate that I'm able to afford things for myself and my family. That's the other side of the coin, and that's where happiness lies.

SCOTT ROSENBERG (Con Air)

I love the excitement of a new idea, of telling the story. I love the whole creative process. Secondly, it allows me to live a life where no day is ever the same. Ever. It's incredible. I have friends who work in a cubicle forty-nine weeks a year, and I don't know how they do it. That's what I love about screenwriting. You get to explore something new all the time.

AFTERWORD

*"We really shook the pillars of
heaven, didn't we Wang?"*
—Big Trouble in Little China

A last word to all who are about to venture off into the world of blockbuster screenwriting.

Always remember those movie screens are big, so keep your dreams big, too. Push yourself to share what's unique and special about who you are and what you care about. Be fearless and bold with your imagination and talent, because that's what the movie audience wants.

But most of all, always strive for a single objective as you create and write your blockbuster screenplay:

Surprise and astonish us all.

RECOMMENDED READING

THE BIG DEAL: HOLLYWOOD'S MILLION-DOLLAR SPEC SCRIPT MARKET
by Thom Taylor, William Morrow and Company

A behind-the-scenes analysis of some of the most famous million dollar spec screenplay deals. It's an informative, insightful, and exciting look at how the game is played by all the key players.

A must read for any beginning screenwriter interested in how it's been done.

ADVENTURES IN THE SCREEN TRADE
by William Goldman, Warner Books

This is the place to start for more insider advice from one of the most gifted and successful screenwriters there is. It's a refreshingly honest and personal account from a long-time veteran who's seen it all.

THE SCREENWRITER WITHIN
by D. B Gilles, Three Rivers Press

Irreverent and funny, but smart, too. This is a terrific screenwriting book written by a friend and colleague. Lots of sharp advice and know-how from a successful writer and master teacher.

HOW TO SELL YOUR SCREENPLAY
by Lydia Wilen and Joan Wilen, Square One Publishers

Everything you need to know about marketing and selling your screenplay. A clearly written and very comprehensive guide that's highly recommended.

LEW HUNTER'S SCREENWRITING 434
by Lew Hunter, Berkley Publishing

Written by a fabled and renowned UCLA screenwriting teacher who's had many students go on to blockbuster careers. This book is a favorite for a very good reason. It's terrific.

THE WRITER'S JOURNEY
by Christopher Vogler, Michael Wiese Productions

Using Joseph Campbell as an inspiration, the author reveals the mythic understructure of stories in a way that's instructive, illuminating, and inspirational. A must read for beginning screenwriters who want to learn the mythic secrets of blockbuster storytelling.

THE GROSS: THE HITS, THE FLOPS–THE SUMMER THAT ATE HOLLYWOOD
by Peter Bart St., Martin's Griffin

Written by the editor-in-chief of *Variety*, this book examines the mega-hits and mega-flops during one action-packed movie summer. A great insider's look at how blockbuster movies are created, assembled, and marketed by a studio machinery that's always hectic and hopeful, but often frozen with fear.

EASY RIDERS, RAGING BULLS: HOW THE SEX-DRUGS-AND-ROCK 'N' ROLL GENERATION SAVED HOLLYWOOD
by Peter Biskind, Simon & Schuster

A magical mystery tour back to the 70s, when wanna-bes like Steven Spielberg, Martin Scorsese, and George Lucas were just starry-eyed kids with blockbuster dreams and goofy hair. They're movie legends now, but back then they were just like you.

THE PSYCHOTRONIC ENCYCLOPEDIA OF FILM
by Michael Weldon, Ballantine Books

 This book is a compendium of every wacky, sloppy, delirious, insane, inept, low-budget, no-budget, and gloriously ambitious bad movie that's ever been shown in a drive-in or on late night TV. There are monsters, meteors, horny teenagers, hot rods, surf music, zombies, prison sluts, giant insects, and lots of shaky spaceships held up by wires flying through outer space. Dive in and swim around. Thousands of bad movies for big-idea inspiration. It's currently out of print but worth hunting down.

ABOUT THE AUTHOR

Sheldon Woodbury is an author, playwright, fiction writer, and screenwriter. He's worked in children's television and written award-winning screenplays. His most recent book is the political parody *W: The First 100 Days, A White House Journal*, written with D. B. Gilles. He also teaches screenwriting at New York University's Tisch School of the Arts, in the Department of Dramatic Writing, one of the top writing programs in the country. He's a graduate of Williams College and has an MFA in Dramatic Writing from New York University.

He can be reached for individual screenplay consultation at: coolscreenplays@aol.com

INDEX